# CREATIVE THINKING HANDBOOK

ANDREW S. BLUESTONE, CFP®

*(Author of Harnessing the Power of Relationships)*

Copyright © 2014 Authored by Andrew S. Bluestone, CFP®
All rights reserved.

ISBN: 0615976654
ISBN 13: 9780615976655

# Creative Thinking Handbook

Andrew S. Bluestone, CFP®, author of *Harnessing the Power of Relationships* shares his thoughts, techniques and tips on how to develop the critical skills necessary for creating and maintaining relationships in business and in our personal lives.

## Table of Contents

Introduction . . . . . . . . . . . . . . . . . . . . . . . . . . . . . . . . . . . . . . . . . . . . . vii

**Section 1 — What is Networking and How Do We Do It?** . . . . . . . . . . . 1

    How Much Do You Know About Networking At Events?. . . . . . . . . . . . 3
    We Are All Connected . . . . . . . . . . . . . . . . . . . . . . . . . . . . . . . . . . . . . 9
    Your Personal Network . . . . . . . . . . . . . . . . . . . . . . . . . . . . . . . . . . . 11
    Wrestling to Find a Network. . . . . . . . . . . . . . . . . . . . . . . . . . . . . . . . 15
    The Learning Cycle. . . . . . . . . . . . . . . . . . . . . . . . . . . . . . . . . . . . . . . 17
    Are You a Natural Networker? . . . . . . . . . . . . . . . . . . . . . . . . . . . . . . 23
    Relationship Capital . . . . . . . . . . . . . . . . . . . . . . . . . . . . . . . . . . . . . . 27

**Section 2 — Developing Skills, Choosing Relationships,**
                **Creating Opportunities** . . . . . . . . . . . . . . . . . . . . . . . . . . . . 29

    Relationship Development. . . . . . . . . . . . . . . . . . . . . . . . . . . . . . . . . 31
    Mastering Small Talk . . . . . . . . . . . . . . . . . . . . . . . . . . . . . . . . . . . . . 35
    Network Nesting . . . . . . . . . . . . . . . . . . . . . . . . . . . . . . . . . . . . . . . . 41
    Just Keep Working It!. . . . . . . . . . . . . . . . . . . . . . . . . . . . . . . . . . . . . 45
    Preschool Advantage . . . . . . . . . . . . . . . . . . . . . . . . . . . . . . . . . . . . . 49

Create an Opportunity for Giving. . . . . . . . . . . . . . . . . . . . . . . . . . . . . .53
Connection Recipe . . . . . . . . . . . . . . . . . . . . . . . . . . . . . . . . . . . . . . . . . .57

## Section 3 — Networking Challenges at Events and In Groups . . . . . . . 61

Interest in Groups. . . . . . . . . . . . . . . . . . . . . . . . . . . . . . . . . . . . . . . . . .63
Networking in Groups . . . . . . . . . . . . . . . . . . . . . . . . . . . . . . . . . . . . .69
Your 30-Second Introduction . . . . . . . . . . . . . . . . . . . . . . . . . . . . . . .73
Successfully Networking at Events . . . . . . . . . . . . . . . . . . . . . . . . . . .77
How to Overcome Networking Hurdles. . . . . . . . . . . . . . . . . . . . . . . . 81
Networking Event Code . . . . . . . . . . . . . . . . . . . . . . . . . . . . . . . . . . .87
Connect and Thrive . . . . . . . . . . . . . . . . . . . . . . . . . . . . . . . . . . . . . . .91
Create a Networking Event . . . . . . . . . . . . . . . . . . . . . . . . . . . . . . . . .93
How to Organize a Networking Event. . . . . . . . . . . . . . . . . . . . . . . . .97

## Section 4 — Maintaining and Organizing Contacts. . . . . . . . . . . . . . . 101

Be a Generator. Learn to Hunt. . . . . . . . . . . . . . . . . . . . . . . . . . . . . 103
The Power of the Unnecessary Letter . . . . . . . . . . . . . . . . . . . . . . . . 105
The Art of Email Introductions . . . . . . . . . . . . . . . . . . . . . . . . . . . . 109
The Power of Intention . . . . . . . . . . . . . . . . . . . . . . . . . . . . . . . . . . 113
Choosing the *Right* Relationships. . . . . . . . . . . . . . . . . . . . . . . . . . . 117
Social Media Networking: 10 Tips for Financial Advisors . . . . . . . . . . 119
LinkedIn Profile Setup. . . . . . . . . . . . . . . . . . . . . . . . . . . . . . . . . . . .125
Marketing Strategies That Work . . . . . . . . . . . . . . . . . . . . . . . . . . . 131
Conclusion . . . . . . . . . . . . . . . . . . . . . . . . . . . . . . . . . . . . . . . . . . . . 135

# Introduction

I first began learning about the power of networking as a teenager in the landscaping business. It was here that I learned the power of relationship development as a means of future business opportunity. It was here that I learned that doing a good job for people would lead to new business. It was here that I learned that being liked and respected are important aspects of building a business. And finally, it was at this stage of my life where I learned that trust and confidence deliver results. I continue to apply these principle throughout my life as a financial advisor and a member of my community.

As the President and CEO of Selective Benefits Groups (a financial services company focused on asset management and educating participants in retirement savings programs) I have recruited and trained over one thousand sales people, coaching them on successfully building their business by developing natural networks. I believe so strongly in the power of relationship building that I recently formed a training company and a website to help professionals harness the power of networking. Visit me at **harnessingthepowerofrelationships.com**.

I truly believe in the adage, *"with age comes wisdom."* Mostly because I am old! My goal in writing this book is to enable readers to recognize the opportunities in their lives, to build stronger bonds in their relationships and to find people who they can serve. Likewise, I have seen steady improvement both personally and through the development of others with whom I have been associated. If I can share what I have learned with just one person and affect their way of thinking

# Introduction

or bring a new perspective and approach to help people manage, grow and begin more significant relationships, my life's pursuit will have served a greater purpose.

My position has remained consistent. This handbook is the result of many years writing about the subject of relationships with a business development slant. My passion and intention for documenting my life's work is only trumped by the time I spend building and developing relationships. Quite a conundrum!

Fortunately I am able to put my thoughts down on paper with the help of Karen Ezzi. Karen has creatively guided my words to meaningful descriptive phrases that created the writing and print results in much of my work.

The content in this handbook is broken down into four sections, which provide real life examples, stories and "how-to" activities that highlight the important aspects of socializing in our chosen networks and offer guidance as you continue your journey toward building enduring and profitable relationships.

1. *What is networking and how do we do it effortlessly?*

2. *How do we develop habits that will translate into skills and ultimately deeper, more significant relationships?*

3. *The challenges surrounding networking at events and in group situations - how to face these challenges head on, overcome our limited beliefs and maximize time.*

4. *Maintaining a robust network takes time, actions and a plan. Each connection is important, categorizing and pruning help provide an updated contact list.*

# Section 1 — What is Networking and How Do We Do It?

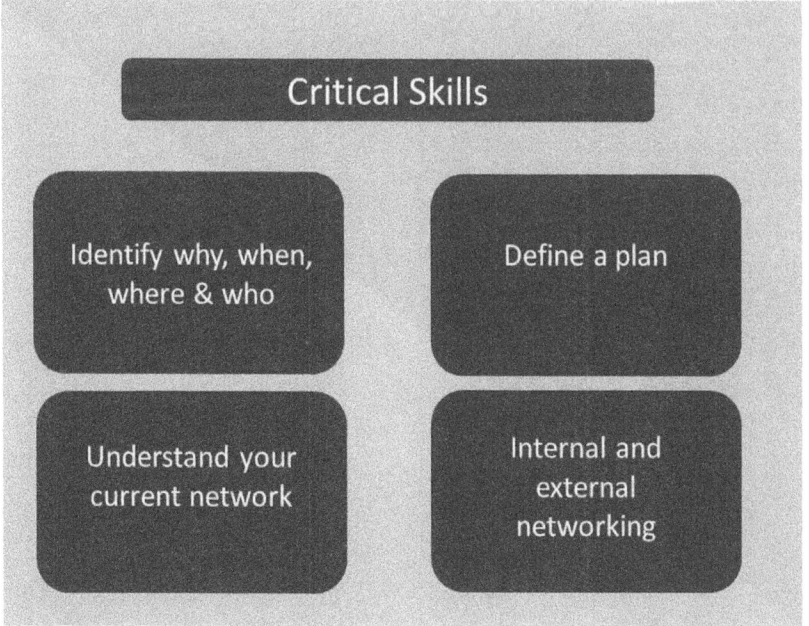

# How Much Do You Know About Networking At Events?

How much do you really know about successful networking at events? This short quiz will help you brush up on your networking skills without having to put on a suit or balance a drink. The answers are at the bottom of the quiz. Good luck!!

**1. When meeting someone at a networking event, you should start conversations with:**

A. casual conversation about the weather, technology, or your dream vacation.
B. your 30-second elevator speech.
C. being inquisitive about their career or why they are attending the event.

**2. When you have a difficult time getting a conversation started or if you are uncomfortable meeting new people, you should:**

A. wait for someone to approach you to begin a conversation.
B. join a small group and gently tap a person on the arm to join the conversation.
C. try meeting people around the food table and talk about how great the caviar tastes.

## 3. The best networkers are those who can:

A. ask other people interesting questions.
B. talk comfortably on a wide range of topics.
C. always pick up the conversation when others run out of things to say.

## 4. The best way to show respect for what someone else is saying is to:

A. compliment them on what they said.
B. ask others to join your conversation to hear what he/she is saying.
C. be a good listener, provide responsive gestures and ask good follow-up questions.

## 5. When preparing for a networking event, you should:

A. ask the host in advance for an attendee list.
B. find out what refreshments will be served, and call ahead for special dietary needs.
C. identify the key sponsors of the event and learn about their business.

## 6. When someone hands you their business card, you should:

A. stick it in your pocket.
B. acknowledge it with a compliment on design or question about the person/company.
C. write notes on the back to refresh your memory later.

## 7. After you have met someone who you would like to spend more time talking to, you should:

A. suggest the two of you excuse yourselves from the event and go to a restaurant or other room where you can talk one-on-one.

B. buddy up with this person and introduce him/her to other interesting people you have met.
C. ask for his/her business card and set a date to meet for coffee or lunch.

**8. If you are networking and someone latches on to you and follows you everywhere, you should:**

A. involve him/her in all of your conversations.
B. tell him/her to get lost.
C. excuse yourself from him/her, indicating that you have set a goal for yourself to meet 5 people at the event and you haven't met your goal yet.

## Answers

**1. A.** While c is appropriate after you have started a conversation, it is considered rude to immediately ask about a person's career. Begin your conversation with casual talk. It's good to have some conversations ready to go. People like to talk about their vacation, the best job they ever had, the one thing they could change about their work/career. Technology is also a good conversation starter. It's all around us: "I see you have an iPhone, what is your favorite gadget?" Learning to be a good story teller is a great way to keep the conversation going. Practice your "go to" story ahead of time. Pick a topic of interest, keep it short, and make sure it's clear and has a message. Stories should be positive, enthusiastic and not mention any names (individuals or companies), unless appropriate. And while having a great 30-second elevator speech is a must-have tool for networking, this is not the time to use it.

**2. B.** As children, we were all taught that we shouldn't talk to (or take candy from) a stranger. Get this out of your head. While meeting new people doesn't appear difficult, it rarely feels that way. Anxieties, social politeness and an unwillingness to get rejected may keep you from taking the first step. These hurdles are really just excuses. These are rules we keep inside our head for when it is and isn't appropriate to meet people. While some of these rules have some basis in reality, most of them are wrong. If you are uncomfortable networking, try this: join a small group already in conversation by gently tapping a person on the arm, offer a quick nod hello, and then focus on the current speaker. They will carry the conversation and frequently introduce you to others to make you feel welcome.

**3. A.** Some of the best conversationalists do the least amount of talking. While b and c are also characteristics of good conversationalists, being able to draw others into the conversation is an advanced networking skill. Be curious. People like to talk about themselves and their successes. Whether it's work achievements, their family, or sports triumphs, most people relish the opportunity to brag a bit. Let them... no, encourage them!

**4. C.** Being inattentive is a common characteristic exhibited by people at networking events. Always display good eye contact with verbal and body language response. Ask good follow-up questions. Networking is more about listening than talking. While most of us are too consumed with *what am I going to say* we are not as worried about being unable to listen. Listening to someone is a form of flattery. Other body language tips to remember: avoid "room grazing", lean forward in interest, smile, nod, say "yes."

**5. A. and C.** If the hosts are willing to share an attendee list in advance you have a great head start. Find out who will be attending the event and identify who you would like to meet. What is the agenda? Are there sessions you should attend and can you carve out some time in between for the sole purpose of meeting people? If you can, try to schedule time with people prior to the event. Don't overlook the event sponsors as possible networking targets. Who are the key sponsors? Are there any reciprocal opportunities or reasons to meet the sponsors that may help your business?

**6. B. and C.** Though it may be habit to take a quick glance and put it in a pocket, it's a flattering gesture to take a moment to recognize and comment on a business card. Remember how much thought and consideration you put into the design of your card? Fortuitously, business cards also provide a great place to make a quick note about the person you've just met or to jot down the date of your upcoming breakfast meeting.

**7. C.** A networking event is more of a social event than pure business. Meet lots of people by spending a few minutes with each. Collect lots of business cards. It's okay to set a date for a follow up conversation or to follow up with a phone call a few days after the event.

**8. C.** It is easy to get stuck with someone who follows you around everywhere you go - especially if you attend an event with a colleague. At some point, find a reason to excuse yourself by explaining your goal to meet many people. Or perhaps introduce him/her to someone and then excuse yourself from their conversation. Don't let another person dominate your time at a networking event.

## How did you score?

### Seven or more correct:
You will be the hit of the party! It is clear you already have strong networking skills and appreciate the value of investing your resources into making new connections. It's guaranteed: you will make some positive contacts, and people will make an effort to get to know you at the next networking event.

### Four to six correct:
You are very close to having all the skills you need in order to really thrive professionally and to enjoy all the personal successes that come from being a skilled networker. With a little effort, you can move to the next level. Practice makes perfect, so get out and network every chance you get.

### Less than four correct:
You'll need some more practice to make the impression you want. Attend an event soon. After the event, reach out to the people you met by phone or email to invite

them to meet for coffee or breakfast. This is the start for making meaningful connections. If you are motivated to learn how to do a much better job making and growing new connections you should consider personal coaching or attend some networking workshops.

# We Are All Connected

*"Everything is connected to everything else."*
— Deepak Chopra

Deepak Chopra best articulates our connection to each other through science and spirituality. My understanding (albeit simplistic) is that bodies are constantly replacing old cells with new ones, at the rate of millions per second – new cells that revitalize our being.

Did you ever wonder where those old, dying cells go? Do they evaporate into thin air or do they become floating particles in the air we breathe? It is scientifically proven that all living things – including plants, insects, animals and our dying cells—eventually become part of the atmosphere. Imagine that we are all breathing, swallowing and absorbing bits and pieces of everyone – every living thing that has come and gone. Think about how the atmosphere creates an enclosed capsule where we are "networked" with each other in the form of atmospheric connectivity.

As Deepak Chopra points out, particles from tyrannical individuals and mass murderers – Osama Bin Laden, Adolf Hitler and Son of Sam – are floating in the atmosphere as we breathe. We are also surrounded by the great lovers of humanity – Gandhi, Nelson Mandela, Mother Theresa and John Lennon.

Our connectivity creates an environment of basic truths. First, we are all connected. Second, humans are all part of an environment and need each other to survive. And finally, our past, present and future are all tied together. Wow... that's heavy stuff! Take a moment to let this sink in. Then, take a deep breath and bring these thoughts down a level.

You may think you are not part of a network. Think again. We are all in a network – actually many networks. The only complicating factor is that our focus on networking is often confused with a negative connotation. We associate it with selfishness – like we are selling something or need to advance ourselves through our network. The simple truth is that our network is not something we create. It is about raising our level of awareness to help others in this human being experience.

Open your eyes. Listen to the sounds and feel the pulses. Reach out to the people with whom you would like to connect. Create a special bond. These connections allow you to follow your passion, give back to those you care for and provide endless opportunities to succeed.

I am certainly not known as, nor do I consider myself, a philosopher. I still believe there are lessons in life and nature that we can and should use to stimulate an awareness which can help us to be more successful in life – and in business—because the two are not mutually exclusive.

Go out networking. Find your place to fill and which pieces connect with your own. Breathe in your greatness.

> *"There are no extra pieces in the universe. Everyone is here because he or she has a place to fill, and every piece must fit itself into the big jigsaw puzzle."*
> — Deepak Chopra

# Your Personal Network

Your personal network lives with you daily. Each of us has a support system which includes family and friends who are supportive of us and us of them.

These people are part of your core network—you've chosen to keep them in your current stage of life and continue to interact with them on a regular basis. These people tend to have a particular role (for example best friend or cousin) in your life where you ideally find mutual support.

Our personal relationships create extraordinary opportunities for growth as individuals because they are not bound by the conventions of etiquette in the same way our business relationships are. There are two main types of people in our personal lives: family and friends.

Family is the only group, with whom you will ever be involved, that cannot be changed. When I refer to family, I am referring to people outside of your household. They are siblings—aunts, uncles, cousins, in-laws, etc. They provide the most important support system in most people's lives.

Family members often work in related industries. For instance, 70% of New York Fire Department members are related to or referred into firefighter positions, by family and close friends. There are unique legacy and recruiting legacy programs.

In my case, my father and I both spent much of our lives in the insurance industry.

Family members may also hold similar positions in other industries such as sales, administrative, education, or accounting.

Naturally, family members with common careers have a support system and inherently will share information. Community and family are often linked too. Family members may participate in the same or related charities, places of worship, and have common community interests.

Taking enough time to understand your relatives and each person's place in the workforce and community will be valuable for career growth. This understanding can lead to opportunities that would otherwise be missed. There is a high level of comfort when talking with family–whether you are an introvert or extrovert–here you can usually let your guard down a bit and know what to expect.

Connections with family are often taken for granted. Nurturing them is an essential element of your personal network. When you are in the company of family members try replace conversations such as, "How are you doing?" with meaningful questions. Find out if you have any business or personal synergies that you might have missed and can help both parties enhance each your lives.

Next time you see Aunt Rita or Uncle Jack try asking something like this, "I know you have been with *ABC Company* for a number of years. You must really like working there. What do you like most about it?" and then listen closely. You will be surprised how much you didn't know about the people you hold dearest and how much you may be able to help each other.

Showing a deeper interest will lead to a higher level of communication and a broader network, which can lead to business or personal growth. Every family is a network full of connections. The richest are those that are cultivated with purpose. Focus with the intent to learn how you can give to those you love.

The other group of personal networks is your friends. After family members, these are your most natural network. Friendship is developed through rapport, trust, common ground and caring—the foundation for any network. Whether friends lend support through good times or bad, these relationships feed the soul at various times of our lives.

Friends tend to rally around you for support when they know you need it. Let them know what you are looking for. You will often be shocked at the response. Remember, your friends have no idea what is going on with you unless you tell them.

Sharing successes with friends can be one of the most rewarding and affirming things you will ever do. All of us like to hear about personal and business growth and this is a subtle way to train them on what works for you. We enjoy each other's success when we are included, especially if we were asked for help.

Years ago I was diagnosed with an acoustic neuroma—not the most common of tumors. As I sorted out my treatment options, nothing was more valuable than my network of friends. My friends were there for support, recommendations, and to offer after surgery care. I spent time talking with a number of my friends who might have some input on the topic. Some helped me get to the best surgeon while others shared books and articles on the topic.

All of this was invaluable in my quest to find the best method to remove the tumor. I found the solution with their help and my friends rallied around me for years with support.

After this experience it occurred to me to create a support system (network) for each part of my life. The various areas of our lives (work, health, interests) are often interrelated and a solid network provides across the board support - people we can call on at any time. Start by creating a list of each aspect of your life - in no particular order of priority.

- career
- hobbies/collectibles/music
- health/personal well-being
- finances
- spirituality
- family
- community interests
- volunteering
- sporting activities

Put the list in column format and add people to each column. This way you can categorize and start calling or writing each person to show your appreciation for the connection and relationship. The response will be surprisingly effective in developing an even greater bond and relationship going forward.

Each time we personally reach out to someone in our network - by giving back or offering help, support, or information - we discover a couple of undeniable truths. We have created a deeper connection, we develop long term relationships, and we expand our network. The act of connecting is 90% of the challenge...the rest takes care of itself.

# Wrestling to Find a Network

My son Dylan is a great example of how joining a group can affect every aspect of your life–often with unintentional rewards. Over the last three years, he has taken up wrestling, as a hobby, to develop a network.

When Dylan was small, he loved community sports programs, particularly soccer, little league baseball, and basketball. I loved attending and coaching his baseball games. I proudly cheered him on as he grew each year into a better athlete and a more supportive teammate.

After years of community leagues, he reached middle school. We saw many of his friends drop out of sports programs as they began to realize their talent was not at the level of some of their peers and the pressure to become "practical" grows stronger. Dylan began to feel some of this stress; he was recognizing that his skills were merely average compared to friends who were beginning to excel in baseball, the sport he preferred.

My family believes in high standards. We established guidelines for our children regarding doing your best in school. Playing an instrument, community involvement, and participating in sports is mandatory. None of my children are star athletes, but all do their best and have always qualified for the teams they chose. Dylan, my youngest, is no exception.

Upon leaving middle school, he proclaimed that baseball would be his sport in high school. He knew the competition was tough. He might struggle to make the team. He knew he might spend his high school years on the bench. Despite all that he wanted to do it. I supported his decision.

My only concern was that the spring baseball season was far away.

To help him acclimate to high school faster, I suggested he become involved with a fall sport while waiting for baseball. He agreed to try wrestling, although unenthusiastically.

Over the summer, he attended a few weeks of wrestling camp. To everyone's surprise, he thought wrestling was a "pretty cool" thing to do!

In all of our excitement, we forgot what years of community sports leagues should have taught us—most high school wrestlers begin training at six or seven years old. Just like other sports. He was behind but undeterred.

A teammate in his same weight class fell to injury. This allowed him to move to the varsity team in his freshman year despite being somewhat behind his teammates. That first year he went 1-26. That means he found himself pinned to the mat 20 times in a public forum, and we won't even go into how many times it probably happened in practice.

My son grew stronger and more resilient, buoyed by his new network of upperclassmen who wrestled with him on the varsity team. Some of my proudest moments as a father were watching how resilient he was while training. He didn't quit, even when everyone would have completely understood if he did.

As a sophomore Dylan's work ethic helped him improve to a record closer to 50/50. Entering his junior year, his strength and mental awareness are sure to bring him greater success.

Beyond the wrestling mat, he is a straight A student. He finds constant support and motivation with the group of teammates he calls friends. I call them part of his network too.

Baseball has faded from Dylan's list of hobbies and wrestling took its place, mostly due to the strong network of friends he made as a beginning wrestler. His teammates help to keep him dedicated and focused. His "network" of fellow wrestlers has now become a positive force as he pursues his future goals and dreams. Dylan has literally been wrestling for a network these past three years!

# The Learning Cycle

Another reason why pursuing things that bring you joy is so important is knowledge accumulation. When you attend an event or join a new network it is important to have an intimate understanding of that network's passion for whatever it is based on. I learned this lesson in 2008 when I worked as a consultant with a biotech company. The CEO is a close friend and an integral part of my business network. Our goal in working together was to build new facilities to extract stem cells.

Basically, adult stem cells can be stored and frozen just like embryonic cells can be. The science isn't quite finished to help rehabilitate completely yet. It's still new. The hope is that someday we may be able to do things like reconstitute a blood stream for someone with leukemia.

You can see that this is complicated stuff, and here I am, with a sales and financial services background trying to network with the scientists and advocates who have sophisticated knowledge that I lacked. It caused me to fall really short of our expectations. It took months just to acquire the essential information needed to hold a decent conversation.

Acquiring that information was not easy for me. It is not my area of expertise or interest.

Do I think it is a phenomenal leap in science that could help millions of people? *Absolutely*.

## The Learning Cycle

Do the ins and outs of this science keep me up at night searching for answers? *No.*

Becoming well rounded and knowledgeable in this area is not as fun as learning about networking or interpersonal relationships which is where my interests lie.

In Malcolm Gladwell's bestselling book *Outliers,* he refers to the mastery of any subject area requiring 10,000 hours of good practice.

Can you imagine spending 10,000 hours on something you are not enjoying completely? The sad truth is people are doing just that. Yet their hours are wasted because it is not enough to just practice. It must be "good or excellent" practice to achieve true mastery. It is next to impossible to perfectly practice something you are not naturally drawn to. I couldn't do it with cryopreservation, even though it was something I believe makes the world a better place.

The experience taught me a profound lesson about why it is so important to follow our passion. The constant training that is needed to rise to a high level of credibility with people in your network can be agonizing if you are doing what you are *supposed* to do instead of following your vision.

Do you have learning or development goals set around the areas that interest you or are you spending all of your time developing yourself in areas that, for whatever reason, you simply are not drawn to?

Networking in communities of like-minded people—all brought together because they find fulfillment in the same arena—is much simpler and more fun than trying to insert yourself into a community that doesn't work for you.

Constant improvement is an essential part of life. Once we've identified what our interests are and how we would like to pursue them, we will want to take the time to learn and practice those skills.

Of course, it then follows that if we want to become exceptional business developers, we will need to educate ourselves and practice our relationship development skills.

Good practices are only developed after we've finished a five-step process: **Realization, Forming Habits, Practice, Mentoring and Mastery.** Think about each of these components individually. Remember, only perfect practice will help you achieve mastery.

1. • Realization
2. • Forming Habits
3. • Practice
4. • Mentoring
5. • Mastery

**Realization** is just what it sounds like. It is the first time we discover a new idea that helps us become more efficient or effective. For instance, if you are new to the concept of strategic relationship development, the idea of setting up a database of everyone you meet is probably new to you. Sometimes those who have already mastered a particular subject have trouble with this idea. They've spent so long improving their skill set that they have forgotten what it is to be a beginner: namely that you simply don't know what you don't know.

Every time you are introduced to a new idea you are likely to encounter one of two reactions—acceptance or rejection. Acceptance comes when you recognize that this knowledge will help you. You feel you can master it. Rejection happens when we are unsure of what the outcome might be or worried that the experience might negatively affect us. That is when your negative brain begins to take over and tell you things like, *I don't have time to record information about everyone!* Pay close attention to those negative reactions, often the new ideas that dredge up the most worry are the things you most need to form new habits around.

**Forming Habits** begins with learning and transformation. It is the internalizing of an idea and the understanding of what it is all about, why it works, and how it applies to your life. Habits are formed as we first explore a new approach and will continue with us as we practice and grow. Habits are formed in three ways which occur at different points in the process.

## The Learning Cycle

In the early stages—when we are just beginning to explore a new idea—learning usually comes in the form of consumption. We read, take classes and Google how-to videos.

As a new networker, you should realize the need to create a relationship database.

Different personalities will require varying levels of information before they feel comfortable moving from consuming to doing. Doing means what you think it does: putting your new knowledge into action.

A networker will start collecting business cards and adding the information to a customer relationship management system. To capture the information on new contacts properly, I always enter the contact within 24 hours of meeting. Remembering to execute this crucial networking step will provide you with more confidence and the more likely the practice is to become a habit that feels natural.

Do note, sometimes research and doing are flipped on their heads. People fall into three categories of learners: visual, auditory, and kinetic. Each will move through this process in a slightly different way. Develop the best system that works for you.

Finally, purposeful new habits continue to develop as we begin to teach others. You might be using a database regularly, and begin talking to others about it. As people follow your example, they will come up with enhancements and new ideas. If a dialog has been created–and since you're using a database to track and maintain a network, it's likely that it has–you will learn new techniques and ideas. Even the process of teaching often teaches us because it opens the door for new and creative ideas in that arena.

Another important habit should be education. The process of forming new habits, and the learning required to do it, never really ends. My own life often feels like one big trip to school. After obtaining my BS in undergraduate school, I went to The College of Denver to obtain my Certified Financial Planner designation. A few years later I studied to become a securities broker. Next, I spent nine years attending classes at Harvard Business School President's Program in Leadership.

**Practice** is where good intentions evolve into lifelong habits. Now that a database system has been identified, use it.

Become really good at asking pertinent questions, being attentive and listening to learn as much as you can about your new contacts. Each time you practice this skill it becomes easier to do the next time.

**Mentoring** happens when we ask for help from someone who has more experience with a particular body of knowledge than we do.

Maybe you are unsure how to apply the information you are collecting. You may choose to seek out resources that can help you. Remember, one day you will be the expert and someone may ask for your help.

Practice and mentoring create a symbiotic relationship. Although mastery is possible without external mentoring, it needs more time, greater frustration, and bigger missteps and failures. An attentive mentor becomes a mirror of our practice. A mentor helps us to develop at a faster pace. Once we've practiced our 10,000 or so hours with the feedback of a master we will reach the final phase—mastery.

**Mastery** is the culmination of years of learning, practice, and mentoring. If Malcolm Gladwell is correct (and I believe he is) then a new networker that spends 10 hours each week actively relationship building would not achieve mastery for nearly three years.

That assumes all practice is excellent, AND many hours are focused on relationship building each week. In reality, it takes most people even longer to truly harness the power of networking.

I offer up this path to mastery not to discourage you, but to start you down the path today and to make sure that you are headed down that path utilizing your strengths and pursuing your dreams. Business development requires a significant commitment to giving and relationship building. It is not an overnight success program. If we begin down the path in the wrong space, like my foray into stem-cell research, we are likely to find ourselves beginning again.

<>

# Are You a Natural Networker?

Yes you are! Networking is a basic skill we all need in order to succeed in life. But when the word "networking" is heard, most people think *I can't do that, I'm quiet, I don't like to sell,* or *I'm a professional.* Yet we all started networking from around the age of two when we first began to speak; it's all about building relationships and the only selling involved is of ourselves and our personality. While it may be simple to walk into a room, it's sure not easy to approach strangers and start talking. It's uncomfortable. It's an unknown. We all have the traits that are found in good networkers but we often don't put energy into identifying these qualities or employing networking behaviors. Let's take a moment and list the traits of a good networker. A good networker doesn't need to own all of them, but as you go through the list, you will start to identify those that fit best with *your* personality.

1. **Consistency.** One of the things that you can count on from masterful networkers is that they are consistent with their networking. They truly live networking. It's their lifestyle. They don't use it as a technique to further their careers. They live their lives such that their networking helps not only them, but also everyone around them. Because networking is an integral part of their lives and their mentality, they don't wait until they have a need to network. They network all the time, so when a need comes along, it's handled almost instantaneously. You will find that it also helps to be consistent in your demeanor and personality. People feel comfortable and learn to trust when they know what to expect.

2. **Knowledgeable.** Do you read the news daily? Stay current with the relevant topics of conversation. For example, at a political convention an expert networker will learn about the politics prior to the event or will learn about the latest models of bikes, etc. when attending a motorcycle rally. Being knowledgeable about the network or event you are involved with doesn't take much homework, but can lead to extraordinary conversations resulting in establishing new and deeper relationships.

3. **Reliability.** Do what you say you are going to do without much fanfare or recognition. Selflessness goes a long way. And, if you say you will do something, do it. Your reputation is critical to future success.

4. **Looks people in the eye.** If you already do this, great. You are respectful and show that you have interest in what the other person is saying. Room grazers not only appear disinterested or self-important, but lack the skills of a good listener.

5. **Masterful listener.** Eye contact is great, but there's more to it than that. When you are a good listener the world of opportunity opens up. For example, you may hear something like: "My firm landed a big account and we are thinking of hiring more staff." Most people will respond with, "Where are you looking to find people" and then continue with a dialogue that may or may not be helpful. Instead, try a new listening technique by mirroring what you have heard. "So your firm landed a big account, congratulations! How did you do this? What were the key factors leading to the big deal?" This is masterful listening gains trust and leads to deeper conversations.

6. **Remembers the facts.** Make a conscious effort to learn more about the people you meet. Ask how the family is by name. Mention what you remember about the individual's work or the last piece of information they shared with you. Showing a sincere interest in others' lives means you will be remembered as someone genuine and caring.

7. **Writes it down.** Keep files and notes for the people that are in your network. Get in the habit of creating a file or journal which can later serve to jog your memory and be used to further develop a relationship. I like to make notes on the back of business cards when I make new connections.

8. **Proactively makes new connections.** Sitting around and waiting for people to approach you at an event, send you an email, or call you on the phone is one of the biggest mistakes of a poor networker. You may have met someone and hit it off or found some commonality. You probably exchanged business cards and now you expect a call. It may not happen…don't stand on ceremony waiting….pick up the phone and set a date for coffee.

9. **Has networking goals.** Identify goals as short, medium and long-term. Once identified, you will be better able to turn your focus and attention outside of yourself. You're more likely, then, to inquire about others' goals and visions and discover mutual ways to be of support. Your conversations tend to be more interesting and compelling. People are more likely to gravitate toward you and want to participate in what you're doing. You tend to attract people who are also goal-centered; therefore, you can generate a network of valuable resources and help one another reach their goals and fulfill their visions.

10. **Be a connector.** Introducing your connections to each other accomplishes two things: 1) being helpful and selfless make us feel great about ourselves, and 2) your network will grow due to your selflessness. You are a connector when you make a direct referral – where someone you know may be in the market for another person's services. Or when you offer a solid contact – an introduction where someone may be helpful to another person down the road.

11. **Is a trusted resource.** Be a resource for everyone you meet. People gravitate to resources. Good networkers who act as a mini advisory board for the people in their network are valued. You may think about

developing a brainstorming session with each person interested in growing. Help them tackle problems and be willing to recommend someone or spend time to come up with a resolution to an issue they may be having. Think through an issue and try to come up with various solutions or ask open ended questions so the other party may be able to answer the questions themselves.

12. **Employs reciprocity.** Some people seem to be natural givers. They like to be of service. They notice others' wants and needs and respond automatically, without being asked. Even if you're not an automatic giver, you can develop a giving nature. It's important to identify what you have that is worth giving. Demonstrate that you can be a resource to others with your professional expertise, external business connections, internal business connections, and community and family connections. We all have our own unique and individual network of friends, family and associates. Very often we uncover something for a friend, family member or associate that needs attention. For example, you may hear someone's mom has a particular illness and is looking for a specialist - you may know someone who can help either directly or through an introduction. You may read a book or an article that may be of interest to someone you know. Pass it on. When you give and become recognized as a giver, it will come back to you in many ways.

13. **Offers advice.** This works for just about anyone in a service-based industry where knowledge is the main product. Give your new connections a couple of ideas specific to your business that may help them in their business or on a personal level. Don't go overboard; maybe share a technique you read in a magazine or tried with one of your clients. This technique opens up a good conversation with the person while you're networking and, if you play your cards right, who do you think they'll go to when they're in need of your kind of service?

# Relationship Capital

You've heard of financial capital, but do you know about *relationship capital*?

Relationship capital is one of the most valuable assets an organization has. It is the international currency of sustainable business growth, especially in business networking. The network of people and organizations that represents customers, partners, suppliers, employees, etc. constitutes an organization's relationship capital. Just like financial capital, relationship capital is accumulated by individuals and used in the production of wealth. It worked for me and I know it has worked for you at times too.

**An Organization's Relationship Capital =
ALL THE RELATIONSHIPS + ALL THE PEOPLE**

Relationship capital is accumulated by providing help, advice, information, referrals, and other benefits to the people you are in relationship with, while not thinking at all about what you'll get back in return.

For most of human history, building relationship capital came naturally, especially in smaller communities. But as small communities grew into cities, the sense of community and the close, personal relationships that went with it, disappeared. A vacuum was created by the disappearance of community-based networking. I've committed my life to teaching business people how to once again develop the strong relationships needed to create sustainable business growth.

The focus of networking should be mainly giving. Connect with others and brand yourself through generosity. Instead of thinking only about what you can gain...or get...from a relationship, think about how you can give. Relationships develop rapidly when you are a giver, and people will remember you. What do you have that is worth giving? Demonstrate that you can be a resource to others with your professional experience, external business connections, internal business connections, and community and family connections. *Give vs. Get*. Pretty unique way of thinking about business growth isn't it?

Understanding your connections needs is equally important. Spending time with someone that you will eventually have a long term relationship with requires a keen ear and acute listening skills. Once we understand someone's desires and personal makeup we can truly help them through possible network and personal connections.

Create systems—through technology and tracking—to help with follow up and follow through to ensure you never forget a name or lose track of a relationship again. If you say you are going to do something, DO IT! If in conversation you say you have a recommendation, or something tangible or intangible that would be helpful to that person, be sure you follow through. Trust is the foundation of your reputation and why people recommend you to others. Relationship capital is a catalyst for building trust with people who don't already know you and while providing opportunities based on your reputation.

All these interactions involve the sharing of knowledge, the solving of problems and the creation of connections. Networking IS NOT about the number of connections you've amassed. Networking IS about the quality of your connections and your reputation with those connections.

# Section 2 — Developing Skills, Choosing Relationships, Creating Opportunities

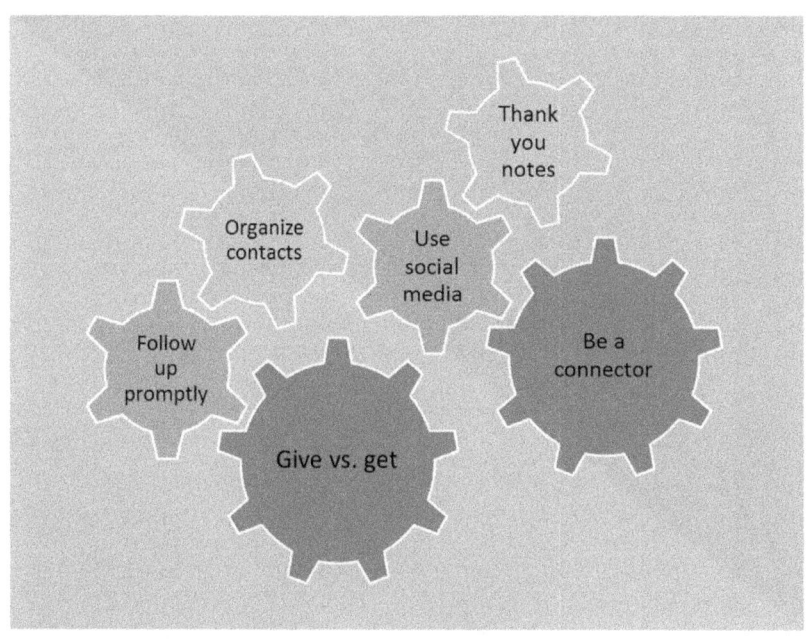

# Relationship Development

**What is a Network?** A network is group of people with links to one another. These links are most common through work, career activities, family, neighbors, friends, community, religion...the list keeps going on. An aspect that clearly defines and differentiates the connections in your network is the support system. People in the same network lend support, give advice, and are available for friendship and help. Think of it as a circle within many other circles that are often connected by influencers who know one another through your network.

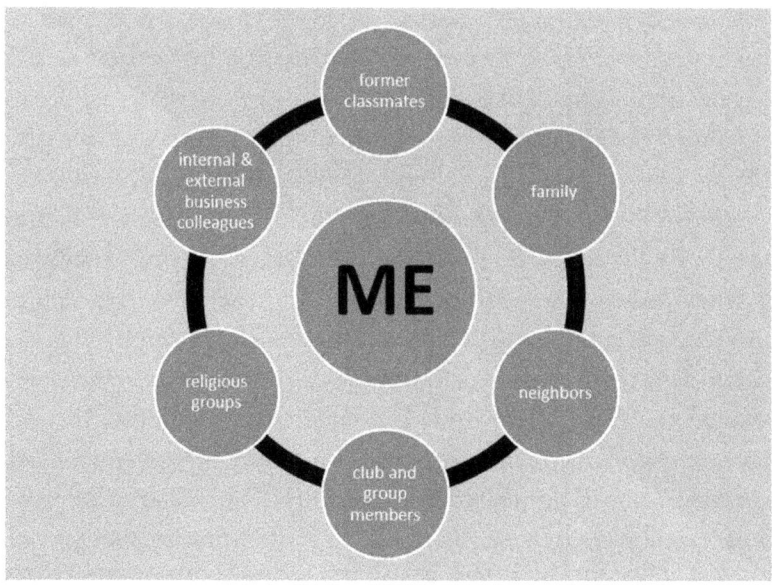

Your network is constantly flowing with the sharing of information, ideas, contacts, and common experiences. The more attention you give to your network, the more powerful the sharing of information becomes...leading to more connections and fulfilling relationships.

Like an atom, a network requires activity to create cause and effect. Activity generates an action that will lead to a chain of movement for all the network members. It starts with communication. Communication fuels the relationships that empowers growth.

The most profound communication comes in the form of being a resource - being proactive by looking for ways to pass along what you know to your network circle. As the center of your network, you have many resources to exchange, share, and pass along to others. Reaching out will strengthen your relationships, enhance the power of the exchange of information, and will lead to more fulfilled experiences in your daily life.

**Introducing People.** Have you ever been in a restaurant with a friend and run into someone you know? Sure you have...and of course, it was natural for you to make an introduction. You just experienced the unintended consequence of a new relationship. The next time this happens, let's say you run into a friend and are introduced to someone with your friend, foster the connection by asking that new acquaintance a few simple questions such as "What do you do for a living?" or "How do you two know each other?" or "Do you live around here?" That introduction can and often will lead to a potential new member of your networking circle. If you are the one making the introduction, take the initiative to add more to further the conversation – like a short background of how you know each other or how the two should get together in the future. Because you are the common denominator for all the people in your network, you have the opportunity to create links between people. Your network becomes even stronger when people in your network know one another and do business or socialize with each other.

**Follow Up.** The exchange of business cards is an important element to networking because it is how people will get in contact with you. Never forget to swap business cards, then follow up with a note or a telephone call. We all appreciate being remembered and recognized. I find it more beneficial to collect business cards verses handing out cards. Some people are better at follow up than others. I know that I DO follow up and having that control leads to better relationship building. I'm not suggesting that you do not hand out your card...but remember to get the card. Make a notation on the card of how you met, who introduced you, and the point of the next contact. For example, you might be having a conversation about restaurants in your neighborhood, so make that note so the follow up is clear and meaningful. If the new acquaintance does not have a card, ask for the email and telephone number and write it down.

To make the most of networking opportunities, here are a few guidelines to follow:

**Characteristics of a good networker:**

1. **Be alert.** Opportunities are all around. Pay attention when someone is speaking, find the common ground or potential growth factor.

2. **Be informed.** Stay current with the relevant topics of conversation. For example, at a political convention learn about the politics prior to the event. When attending a motorcycle rally, learn about the latest models of bikes, etc. Being knowledgeable about the networking event you are attending doesn't take much homework, but can lead to extraordinary conversations resulting in establishing new and deeper relationships.

3. **Listen more than you speak.** There is a reason we have two ears and one mouth. Listen and be ready to act on opportunities where you might be able to help someone. Smile when listening. Don't look away when you are spoken to and stay alert while engaged in conversation. Your attitude and attentiveness are evident each and every time we engage in conversation.

4. **Be consistent.** You will find that it helps to be consistent in your demeanor and personality. People feel comfortable and learn to trust when they know what to expect.

5. **Be respectful.** When we treat others the way we expect to be treated, we gain respect and can leverage that respect to form a more powerful network of trusted connections. Be considerate. Each of us has personal preferences. Though we may not always agree on specific ideas, it is vital to respect someone's point of view.

Be aware of the network you already have and how vast and powerful it can be when utilized effectively. Because of the many strengths, skills, information, contacts, and expertise that you have to offer others (and that others have to offer you), your network can generate a multitude of opportunities for yourself and others. Building relationships takes skills that we all possess. Building relationships is also habitual. The habit of giving and growing your network becomes easier the more you interact and work on it. We know that networking is about making connections but an obvious, and often overlooked point, is that networking is also about building enduring, mutually beneficial relationships.

# Mastering Small Talk

The list of excuses is endless:
"I'm not good at small talk."
"I don't know what to say."
"I don't have anything interesting to talk about."

Do you say this? Does this sound like you? Don't worry, you are not alone. Many intelligent and interesting people are not comfortable with small talk. They feel like they never know what to say and have little value to contribute. Learn how to put these discomforts aside and master the simple art that is small talk.

When someone asks, tell the truth. Yes, the truth. Sometimes that really opens the door for deeper more meaningful conversations. Small talk can become intimate quickly if we use thought provoking questions and display actual concern because people really do like to talk about themselves!

When we are relationship developing (we are pretty much doing this all of the time) the goal of small talk is only to bring us to the point of scheduling the next meeting or moving on. Over the years, I have developed a ten step format to help you be comfortable when meeting new people because you will always know what to say. Creating a bond may produce a next meeting.

I suggest practicing these steps in your office or at home before going out to your next event. Let's take a look at how each one works.

**1. Prepare.**
Take a few minutes before the event to identify a few topics that relate to the event or the individuals you are going to meet. Once you have these topics in mind, it will be easier to speak and to ask others their thoughts or experiences because you have confidence in these areas.

If you don't know enough about the event you are attending, a few other topics that are almost universally relatable are: children, travel plans, family, personal health, and homeownership. Remember our first lesson on being yourself.

**2. Seek out common ground.**
Finding common interest with someone helps to solidify the link. Common interest will bridge the gap between strangers. Look for shared interests if they are not readily apparent. Topics such as where you went to school, sorority or fraternity affiliations, charities, or hobbies you are involved with will all help you do that.

**3. Expand and seek.**
Most people do not go alone to an event. Many only speak with people they know after they get there. Staying in your inner circle will not help to expand your network. Look for someone who appears unsure. This may be the perfect way for both of you to practice networking skills.

**4. Listen.**
When you are engaging in conversation, be attentive and curious. Ask lots of questions with the goal of finding something interesting in the answer. Make eye contact as much as possible. Most people spend so much time thinking about what to say next that we do not actively listen. Ask questions to demonstrate your interest and thorough attention. This will help you to create a rapport with the person with whom you are talking.

## 5. Listen louder.

Show your interest in the conversation. Use your body language, such as nodding and leaning in, to demonstrate this. This is where a conversation method called "mirroring" is particularly useful. It is the verbal equivalent of looking at the other person in the mirror and is really simple to do. Every time the person you're talking with answers a question, paraphrase it back to them. It goes like this:

>"Mr. Smith, what is your biggest challenge in your business?"
>
>"Finding the right employees is really challenging for me. I'd say that is my biggest challenge."
>
>"So you have a hard time recruiting great talent for your team?"
>
>"Not the whole team, I just can't seem to find a secretary who knows how to use Excel."

See how this technique works to make sure we understand exactly where our conversation partner is coming from? When you display greater attention, the speaker will share more freely. Be sure to remember those follow up questions! Bonus points if you can paraphrase what the person just said as you do this.

Be open and honest with your reactions. People know the difference between real interest and feigning.

## 6. Ask questions.

Pose non-threatening questions as part of your curious interest. For example, someone might say that one of his children has an illness. Your curiosity might lead to help solving a problem through one of the contacts in your network. Finding a place in the discussion to take it to the next level could prove to be a turning point in the relationship. You will want to stop and consider how you approach this before diving in. Don't offer advice or resources too early in the conversation. Ask enough probing questions to gain a level of trust first.

## 7. Avoid conversation pitfalls.

While it may seem obvious to avoid the topics of religion and politics, remember to be careful about remarks that could be considered objectionable by others.

In general, steer clear of jokes—what one person finds amusing, another may find offensive or not understand. Avoid making people feel inferior through the use of industry jargon, or phrases like, "Well everybody knows that..." Never make demeaning comments about others, especially your competition. As your mother would remind you, talking about others only makes us look bad. It is necessary to remain positive and non-judgmental.

**8. Persist.**
Don't give up on a conversation if it starts out slowly. Some people are more difficult to break through to than others and everyone adjusts to social settings at their own pace. Think about how uncomfortable you might feel and understand that the other person is probably feeling just as uncomfortable if not more. If a conversation stalls, throw out a few different kinds of topics—something is likely to click.
If you find yourself completely stalled mid-conversation try this technique: share something that has happened to you recently or a memorable moment from the past. Then pause and give the person you are talking with time to make a thoughtful reply. Think of it like speaking with your children about what they did at school today, sometimes it takes a few probing questions to get the conversation moving, but pretty quickly it can turn into a vivid story. Your willingness to communicate may spark something in the other person.

**9. Follow up.**
When a rapport exists, you will know it. The feeling of discomfort will have given way to a sense of ease. You may even feel this in your body, as the tension in your shoulders relaxes.
You will recognize that a connection has been made. This is where small talk has reached the level of *real talk* and business cards should be exchanged. Create a plan to follow up by phone, email, or a date on the calendar for coffee. Then, make sure to make your follow up call or email within 48 hours.

**10. Move.**

Once you have engaged in conversation with someone, developed a rapport, committed to following up, and exchanged cards it is time to move along and meet someone new! Find another person who appears to be uncomfortable and start the process all over again. Kudos to you if you take this to the next level and follow these ten steps with a group that has already engaged in conversation. Strive to stick with this format and do not attempt to go deep into a conversation at an event. Save that for the next meeting.

Small talk is the precursor to making a connection and expanding your network. It leads to trust and rapport in a future relationship. When common interest is found, congratulations! You have just expanded your network!

> *"Eighty percent of success is showing up."*
> — Woody Allen.

# Network Nesting

Network nesting is about finding the common ground among various groups in similar businesses. It is an advanced networking strategy where efforts are focused on a narrowly defined group within a particular industry. Rather than a larger, general audience, these "niches" offer opportunities for you to establish yourself as an expert and "go to" person for the products and services you offer. In identifying a networking nest and learning about the specific needs of these businesses, you can customize your products or services to best to meet the needs of a very small section of the market.

Network nesting is a skill that may take years of experience to develop. The time required to nurture and develop a networking nest will divert focus from other areas of your business. Be sure to choose a nest where your experience and expertise have value and allocate your time carefully.

Evaluate your interests, skills and product/service offerings. Then, identify the needs, wants and requirements of your targeted clients. Once you have identified a niche, test its success by meeting with one or two prospects to gauge the opportunities and potential for income. After all, in order to be successful, a business needs to make a profit!

When I was selling life insurance products in my early 20's, I spent my first year in the garment district of New York City. I was able to move from business to business - men's clothing to women's clothing to children's clothing, to shoes – all within four square block radius in NYC. This made it easy for me to call on hundreds of companies. The following year, I moved to the accessories area in fashion – scarves, belts, and hats – all at the Empire State Building. I was able to spend my days in one building with seventy-five floors and over one hundred companies in one location! I uncovered the commonalities among the businesses there and spent time speaking with these potential clients to gain an understanding of their specific needs and concerns. With this information I was able to develop an expertise in their industry and soon became a trusted resource.

A few years later I worked the meatpacking district in the lower Manhattan. Meats were a small but intimate market. The cow, pig, deer and wild game purveyors were extremely friendly competitors due to supply and demand and were tremendously supportive in helping me make connections within their sphere of influence. The close proximity and similarity of the businesses enabled them to become resources to each other and, as I became known as an expert provider, I benefitted from many referrals within the nest.

# Example of Nesting:

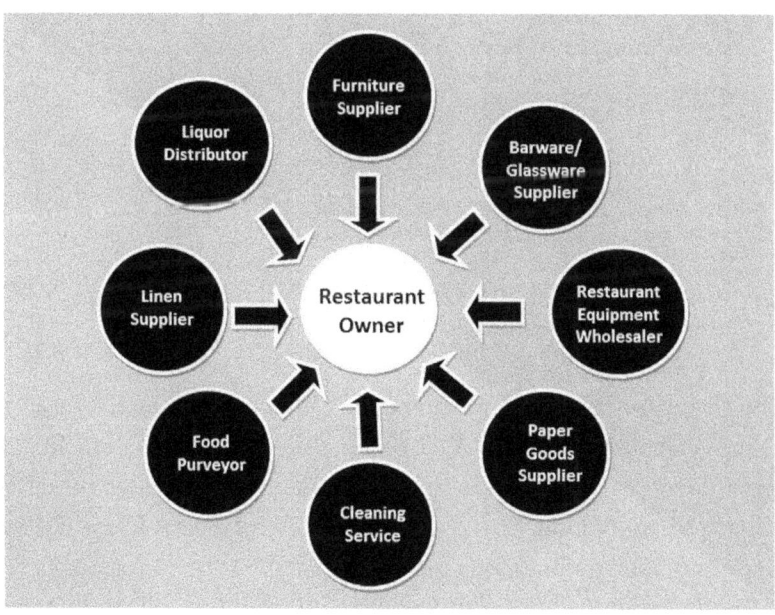

How can you become a great nesting networker? After you identify the industry, gain an understanding of the needs of that nest, and clearly establish ways your business can fit into it, then start networking.

Example of Nesting:

Here are some tips that can help:

1. When gathering referrals, be specific as to whom you would like to meet in a network of people that know each other and have common interests.

2. Give the referrer names to help identify who they may know and be able to introduce you to.

3. Referral gathering should be at the beginning of the sales cycle, not the end. Be aggressive early on in the relationship - describing for the customer how referrals from happy clients are the only way your business grows.

4. Create a plan with the amount of expected referrals you expect to gather each week. Target the ones that are most likely to become good clients.

5. Be prepared to provide your referral sources quality leads to help them grow their own businesses too.

The advantage of finding nests and developing your business there is that you create relationships where YOU become the expert in your field. All the members of the nest will consider you the "go to" person for the products and services you are promoting. Immerse yourself in their industry and you'll become the expert they look to for proven solutions.

<>

## Just Keep Working It!

*"You get a lot of benefit from giving, not taking. You fill a void, give people something that's meaningful and useful."*
— Russell Simmons co-founder of DEF Jam Records.

Two years ago I met Justin. He is a young, intelligent business person and we hit it off instantly. We found we could relate personally and have certain synergies that could lead to growth in our respective businesses. We both recognized that it would take time for our relationship to develop. That was the unspoken awareness and long term opportunity.

We were introduced at a meeting of an organization where we are both members. The key to getting to know each other well was the leadership position I occupied in the organization. My role is to bring in new members and help them assimilate quickly into small forum style groups that create a real growth opportunity for each member. Being part of an organization is one thing, serving as a leader is whole other story! The members look up to the leader in every way and I have an inherent obligation to be a resource and mentor to new recruits. However, this doesn't mean that my participation in the organization is purely selfless because I am, of course, meeting people and making connections to develop my own business opportunities. I have always believed in "give vs. get" and my leadership position easily lends itself to giving to members before I expect to gain anything in return. It's not about me and it's all about them.

The focus of networking and building relationships should be mainly on giving. Instead of thinking only about what you can gain...or get...from a relationship, think about how you can give. Relationships develop when you give and people remember you. I believe there are three very important components to this theory.

The first factor is time. Spending time with someone that you will eventually have a long term relationship with also requires a keen ear and acute listening skills. Once we understand someone's desires and personal makeup we can truly help them through possible network and personal connections. What can I do to help someone grow their business? Are there any problems I can help to solve? I offer help and strategies out of kindness and because I am truly interested in a person and his/her success. Any gain that comes my way is simply a by-product of my genuine interest. However, building relationships – of any kind – is not something that happens overnight. In my opinion, a solid relationship takes at least a year. When I meet someone at an event, a group, or a club, I know it takes time to develop a business relationship. We all know we are there for the same reason, but also know that it takes time. How strange would it be if I was introduced to someone for the first time and immediately asked for his business? My impression of such a person would be aggressive and impolite. Be sure to contact people when you are NOT in need of something. Take time to learn about their business since it's as important to them as your business is to you.

Second, it is important to identify what you have that is worth giving. Demonstrate that you can be a resource to others with your professional expertise, external business connections, internal business connections, community connections and family connections. We all have our own unique and individual network of friends, family and associates. Very often we uncover something for a friend, family member or associate that needs attention. For example, you may hear someone's mom has a particular illness and is looking for a specialist - you may know someone who can help either directly or through an introduction. You may read a book or an article that may be of interest to someone you know. Pass it on.

And third, become an advocate. When I have taken the time to truly know someone and understand their business and what they are trying to achieve, our relationship moves to the next level. I become an advocate for someone when there is trust, understanding of needs, and a desire to further the relationship. It's a level of trust and comfort. I look for opportunities where I will actually refer them to someone who I think could help their business - especially where I have nothing to gain. People really appreciate it when they realize that you're looking out for them. And vice versa. Our business relationship is rooted in the fundamentals of what makes for good people connections: mutual respect.

Getting back to Justin...... We have invited each other to sporting, business and charitable events, he has become a valuable member of the forum group we participate in together and I have referred him to a few business and personal opportunities. We have become friends and a trusted resource for each other.

The reality is that business relationships are just like any other. They require some effort to maintain and they must be mutually beneficial. You must be willing to give, share and support, not just take or receive. A relationship is something you need before you know you need it. In other words, develop contacts and connections for the right reasons—even if they are purely business-based—not just because you want to sell something. Networking for business reasons takes time, commitment and sometimes, patience.

# Preschool Advantage

In 1993 two respected businessmen in my community approached me to help start a new non-for-profit charity. Their idea was simple and had the potential to make an enormous impact in our community. The concept excited me enough that I decided to check it out. I am so glad that I did. The organization touches my heart and has become a great contributor to following my passion of helping people be the best they can be.

One of my networking and relationship development methods for success is to never say *NO* when asked to participate in a cause or business in an area of passion. Just say *YES*, all the time.

I learned early on that one of the most effective ways to do this is to start early in life, by helping children with their education. My passion for seeing a new generation succeed has kept me motivated and focused in my charitable efforts for years. After all, even generosity needs focus to allow you to have the greatest impact possible.

We are focused on helping underprivileged children—those living close to poverty—jump start their education by working with community partners to give each child the opportunity to attend preschool. This is commonplace today, but in 1993 many young children did not have this valuable opportunity.

The target groups of children typically come from working single-parent families. These children often spend a lot of time watching television while their mother or father works hard to support the family. The goal of helping these children is to help them get to preschool. This establishes an educational tone for the rest of their lives, rather than allowing them to start kindergarten already behind their more affluent peers.

We first developed the infrastructure by working with clergy in our community to identify families in need. Then, we approached local businesses to help fund the program and spread the word. Once we obtained support from these and a few other passionate members of our community our initial eight supporters easily multiplied to 24.

We then approached preschools within 10 miles of our headquarters—my office in those days—and gained commitments for one or two full tuition scholarships or reduced tuition programs.

Selecting the children was the most complicated piece of the puzzle. We chose a child selection committee dedicated to interviewing the children, their parents and the pre-schools, in order to set up a perfect fit for each child.

Finally, after all this organizing, a fundraising committee had to be formed. We never imagined that raising funds for kids would be so difficult! We did not realize there were already so many other local charities tied to education and working to gather funds. It sure wasn't easy in the early stages before we proved our model.

In the first year, we raised $7,800 and sent five children to preschool. We were operating out of my office with supplies I donated. By our fifth year, we had enrolled 32 children with a $230,000 budget. This was quite an accomplishment by itself and unprecedented for what happened next: We were approached by the Geraldine R. Dodge Foundation.

With the foundation's commitment, promoting critical and creative thinking for young people in under-served communities, we drew their attention and were a perfect fit. The collaboration put us on the map.

Through the generosity of each person involved in the construction of our organization, we created a structure for creating impactful organizations that I have used ever since. We first identified a need congruent with our talents. Then, we went into the community and found influencers who felt passionate about that need as well. Next, we lobbied for sponsors and enlisted the help of key partners to provide support and PR for the initiative. Finally, we began to seek out clients who would eventually become advocates for our organization when they experienced success through our program.

The creation of this charity illustrates networking in its ultimate form: strong relationships with the primary goal of giving.

I developed life-long friendships with most of the key board members and several local business leaders. Over the years, we have shared vacations, dinners, and business opportunities. Even our children have developed deep friendships with each other. We became a closely knit group that began with the dream of giving back to children in our community.

The simple act of giving first is the single most important mindset transformation that you will need to build your business and follow your passion through relationship development.

What does generosity really mean? I think in America we have too narrow a view of it. We think of generosity as giving money or time to charity, and certainly it is. True generosity is much deeper than that.

I share with you what we accomplished in creating a charity not to put my financial contributions or the time commitment or even the achievement on display. Instead, I want you to see what the crucial element here really is: that giving of yourself, means a willingness to share your passion and your own unique gifts, sometimes to the point of vulnerability.

We had big dreams when we started this organization. If we failed, it would mean hundreds of children miss out on the opportunity to have a better life. Everyone involved, especially at those all-important early stages gave of themselves to the point of vulnerability and sometimes even a little pain. That is why we succeeded and why we built relationships that last a lifetime.

We too often compartmentalize our lives into business and charity. We make the mistake of becoming frazzled or hungry or ambitious which causes us to go into new situations, whether a lunch with a partner or out to an event, with the question of *What am I going to get out of this?* first in our minds. Of course, we must ask for the things that we want, and not at the expense of true generosity.

We should go into every conversation and interaction with the primary goal of helping someone else get what they want.

Without a doubt, my personal and business life are far better today due to the simple act of giving....

# Create an Opportunity for Giving

Most of us are looking for the next opportunity. We know we must keep the pipeline full; the efforts to fill the pipeline today will eventually result in new business. "How do I get new business?" "How do I get a meeting with so-and-so?" "How can I get this account/promotion/job?" And so on. It never stops. It's a continuous loop of need where we are always thinking about what's next.

We need to get out of this on-going conundrum of always hunting. To counter this mentality, we must adjust our thinking from *what can I get?* to *what can I give?* Instead of worrying about getting that meeting, how can you give back to that person? How can you create value?

Giving is a strategy. The focus of building relationships should be mostly on giving. It's about creating value so you don't need to get anything in return. You create an environment of giving not because you feel obligated but because it makes sense. Giving takes the focus off of yourself. You will find that giving reduces stress and changes your perceptions in a positive way, allowing you to build stronger relationships. Being a giver doesn't mean that you are giving stuff away. You are not providing your services or offering your products for free. Giving means that you are taking an interest in the people you are trying to reach. When you focus on giving, the getting doesn't seem so important. Relationships develop when you give and people remember you. I believe there are three very important components to this strategy.

The first factor is time. Spending time with someone that you will eventually have a long term relationship with also requires a keen ear and acute listening skills. Once we understand someone's desires and personal makeup we can truly help them through possible network and personal connections. *What can I do to help someone grow their business? Are there any problems I can help to solve?* I offer help and strategies out of kindness and because I am truly interested in a person and his/her success. Any gain that comes my way is simply a by-product of my genuine interest.

However, building relationships – of any kind – is not something that happens overnight. In my opinion, a solid relationship takes at least a year. When I meet someone at an event, a group, or a club, I know it takes time to develop a relationship to get business. We all know we are there for the same reason, but also know that it takes time. How strange would it be if I was introduced to someone for the first time and immediately asked for his business? My impression of such a person would be aggressive and impolite. Be sure to contact people when you are NOT in need of something. Take time to learn about their business since it's as important to them as your business to you.

Don't expect to make connections that bring value to your business development efforts overnight. It takes time to develop meaningful relationships and mutual trust. Cultivate your new relationships by sending your email newsletter (with permission) or offering an invitation for coffee or a lunch date. There's no need to invest a lot of time developing your new relationships, it's more important to develop a continuous stream of contact. And remember to give first. If you can bring two connections together - great! If you can share an article or some other pertinent information - pass it along. It's about the number of 'touches.' Give it at least a year to really see results from your involvement in networking groups.

Second, it is important to identify what you have that is worth giving. Demonstrate that you can be a resource to others with your professional expertise, external business connections, internal business connections, and community and family connections. We all have our own unique and individual network of friends, family and associates. Very often we uncover something for a friend, family member or associate that needs attention. You may read a book or an article that may be of interest to someone you know. Pass it on. If you can't solve a problem, you can be a connector. Referrals to other people in your network might be a possible strategy. The benefit of this approach is twofold. First, you'll be seen as a problem solver, and second, those people who benefit from your referrals are more likely to provide you with referrals in return.

And third, become an advocate. When I have taken the time to truly know someone and understand their business and what they are trying to achieve, our relationship moves to the next level. I become an advocate for someone when there is trust, understanding of needs, and a desire to further the relationship. It's a level of trust and comfort. I look for opportunities where I can connect two people when I think they may be of help to each other - especially where I have nothing to gain. People really appreciate it when they realize that you're looking out for them. And vice versa. Our business relationships are rooted in the fundamentals of what makes for good people connections: mutual respect.

This may sound like feel good nonsense, but the reality is that business relationships are just like any other. They require some effort—actionable steps to maintain and they must be mutually beneficial. You must be willing to give, share and support, not just take or receive. A relationship is something you need before you know you need it. In other words, develop contacts and connections for the right reasons—even if they are purely business-based—not just because you want to sell something.

# Connection Recipe

Through trust you build relationships.

Have you ever baked a cake from scratch? Then you'll understand the importance of precision and careful adherence to a recipe needed to produce a show-stopping dessert.

Julia Child's famous Chocolate Almond Cake has thirteen ingredients, requires ten pieces of equipment, and takes nearly three hours to prepare—one misstep during the process, and the cake is nothing but a murky brown mess. Baking is pure science for all but the most fluent masters. Step out of line and disaster strikes. To become a good baker, you must practice precision and patience.

On the other hand, cooking a great meal requires a little of something more difficult to define. You may have experienced this when trying to replicate a favorite family recipe. No matter how perfectly you follow that recipe for Grandma's lasagna, something is missing.

There is an art to the blending of flavors and balancing of spices necessary to become a great cook. It cannot be easily taught. It must be experienced. Learn the rules and then learn when to break them. Study techniques and then learn to create your own flavors. To become a great cook you must learn the techniques and then release your unique personality.

Relationship development is a lot like cooking. Learning the right techniques for networking and relationship development will give you a sound foundation. To harness the power of relationships you must embrace the art in it.

Traditional sales training ignores relationship development techniques as a way to grow a business. Traditional training programs are concerned with the process, activity, and production that don't necessarily lead to relationship development measurement. Traditional training is more like baking a cake than cooking a delicious dinner. Both are satisfying and rewarding, but you can't live on dessert alone!

At the beginning of my career as an insurance agent I targeted the meatpacking district of 1980's era New York City. During that time, I learned a thing or two about the recipe for a successful business and a fulfilling life. Lessons like the importance of presentation. It only took me a few days to notice that while all the meatpackers wore bloody white coats, it was only the food inspectors (and probably the IRS) who wore suits. The apprehension of a passing grade was definitely not the first impression I was going for. I learned my first lesson on branding—I needed to leave the suit at home and buy a few more pairs of jeans. As a young businessman I also learned lessons about the power of networking nests and common interest. But most of all, I learned that confidence, determination, and a dedication to helping others will always win in the end.

If you've taken the time to learn to cook, the kitchen becomes an oasis. Somewhere you can move about, throwing in a dash of pepper here or a cup of cream there, always trusting your intuition, knowing that you're creating something delicious. Once the habits are formed, the art and joy take over.

The same thing is true about relationship development. Once you form the right habits, it becomes an art that doesn't feel like work. You are literally building your business while enjoying other people! What could be more natural? What could be more rewarding?

The power of business and a life built on relationship development is that the more you pursue your passion, the more you connect with others who share it, the more you bring people together, the more you grow. Imagine the possibilities to shape not just a successful business, but a fulfilling life!

That power is yours to harness. Remember, you are networking all the time. You are building relationships all the time. You are developing your business all the time. Be clear. Make careful word choices. Make eye contact. Listen.

Communicate. Personalize even the briefest interactions. By doing these things, you will continually build connections and foster stronger relationships.

All of the skills needed for networking and business development boil down to a few things: respect, trust, and confidence with the people you choose to surround yourself with. The more trust that exists within our relationships, the more fruitful they will be—not just for you, but for everyone around you.

# Section 3 — Networking Challenges at Events and In Groups

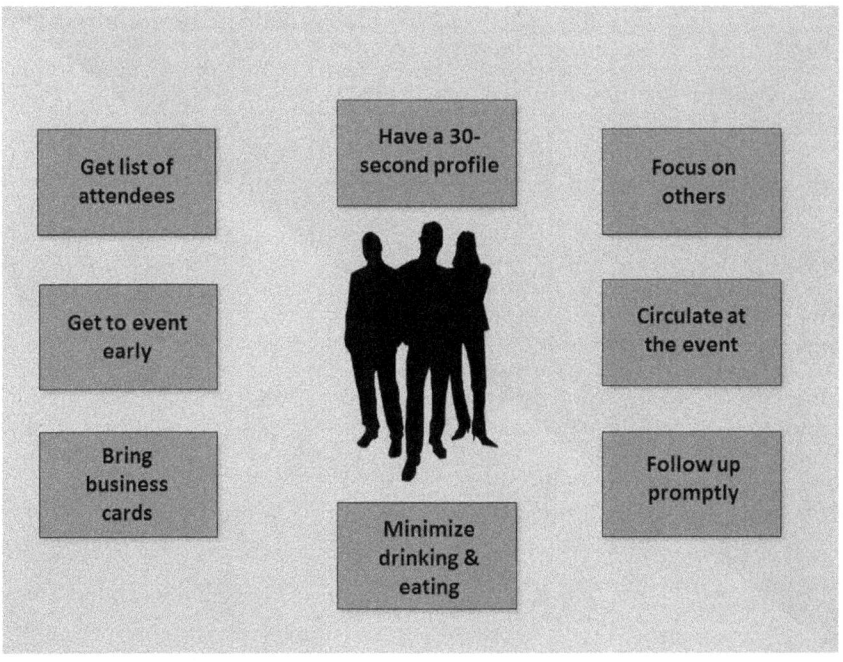

# Interest in Groups

Building relationships can often feel like a constantly moving target--an occasional lunch, a run-in at the grocery store, an after work cocktail all happening fairly sporadically. The best way to build relationships, provide structure, and gain exposure quickly is to become involved in groups that serve your business and/or your passion.

These groups come in many forms—some you might be familiar with like Rotary Clubs or Chambers of Commerce. Others will be new to you. Did you know there is an International Tuba Players Association? It's true! These groups will become the pillars of your weekly or monthly relationship development calendar, allowing you to spend a few hours gaining exposure with dozens of people who all share similar interests and objectives to yours.

Over the years I have participated in many types of groups. I have continued to participate in some and others I quickly found were not a good fit for me, my business or my interests. Below are some tips that will help you to explore how to choose the right groups and how to interact within them to achieve the greatest success.

Choosing the right group to join is essential to establishing the right kind of connections. By beginning with a good-fit, you lessen the chances of frustration and improve the likelihood that spending time with the group will be time well spent. Follow these five steps for choosing a group to join and you will know that it is the right one.

**1. Search for groups based on your objectives.**
Before beginning to search for a group, think about what you want to accomplish and what types of groups are likely to help you reach those goals. For example, if you're looking for a group specifically to build your business, without the need for a lot of social development first, you'll want to choose an organization around your industry rather than a charitable organization.

A plumber might choose to join a realtor's association instead of a Rotary group. Both groups are terrific networks but come together to achieve vastly different purposes. One is a linear group, chosen to help mine a vein of referrals and the other is a community organization designed to help the world. Understanding why you want to belong to the group will help you choose an organization that works for that goal.

Carefully consider professions that are not a part of your network already. Creating relationships with a particular type of professional/person to round out your network is another great way to choose a group to interact in.

Remember that you will probably be pursuing several different goals surrounding things you are interested in. This will lead to involvement in many different organizations so don't feel like you are restricted to just one.

I've spent time in Rotary Clubs, a Young Presidents Organization (YPO), Chambers of Commerce, professional associations, charitable organizations, and hobby clubs over the years; usually belonging to a few different groups at any given time. This is a good idea. As you move in and out of organizations, become a connector by making introductions and referrals among the relationships you have in different groups.

**2. Have a real reason to get involved.**
Once you've identified your personal goals, and chosen a few groups to look at, take the time to think about the first rule of relationship development. First start with giving. Knowing what you can give to the group and how you will be able to help them—at least in a vague sense—should be a high-priority when choosing an organization.

When considering what you can give, do not go in with the tunnel vision of thinking purely about business. Think of ways you can contribute to the group in at least these three categories: helping, connecting, and leading. By approaching the group from the position of a giver instead of a taker, you will set yourself apart from every other candidate who walks through the door looking for the next big fish.

**3. Understand the group's expectations and conduct your own interview.**
At my first meeting with the YPO Board, I made it my business to learn as much about the board members as possible.

I was there to be interviewed. I knew this room full of people held a wealth of knowledge and I could learn much from them. I wanted to know what their motivations and how YPO benefited them.

Instead of spending a lot of time answering the questions of a bunch of intimidating people (remember, at this point they were all more successful than I was), I became the interviewer. Building relationships in groups necessitates even more upfront understanding than attending an event.

You are making a long-term commitment when joining a group and should be clear about what the organization wants from you, what you can contribute, and what the requirements are.

Ask yourself and others these questions:

- *What other types of people are members?*
- *Who do I know who is already a member?*
- *Who do I want to meet?*
- *When are the meetings?*
- *Do they fit with my schedule?*
- *Is there an attendance requirement?*
- *Is there a dress code requirement?*
- *What is the agenda (ex. is the organization primarily structured or mostly mixers or education or a combination)?*
- *Who are the key leaders and influencers?*
- *Does the group offer education to its members or is it more socially or community oriented?*
- *What are the rules and policies for members?*

- *What is the true cost of being a member? (Not just the dues and event fees, but the time commitment as well.)*
- *Who would benefit from attending with me?*

After answering these questions, you should have a crystal clear vision of what the organization is trying to be. Hopefully you will have a rough vision of how you can help the group and how it will help you pursue your passion. Once these objectives are clear you can move on to assessing how the organization fits for you.

**4. Decide if the group fits your style and your goals. Both matter.**
In a business development utopia, we would always encounter organizations that help us to meet our objectives and fit really well with our personalities too. Often that isn't the case. We encounter a vertical organization within our industry that can help introduce us to thousands of referrals, and might be more conservative or less structured than we like. Or, we find a charitable organization that touches our heart and is full of dedicated and unique individuals, but isn't pursuant to something we are truly passionate about. At this point, we must weigh personal fit against our objectives from the business development and passion pursuing goals we have set for ourselves.

**5. Attend one or two meetings before committing.**
The final step in choosing an organization to join is to sample what a meeting or event is truly like. A website or an over-zealous member can say anything, and until you've seen for yourself it is never a sure thing. If at all possible, be a guest before becoming a member so that you can evaluate the strengths and weaknesses of the group dynamic for yourself.

While visiting the meeting, take time to speak to the members about their experiences in the group. Ask probing and open ended questions about what the member has given, learned, or gained as part of the group. Look for clear leadership and direction. Try to figure out who the influencers are. These people are often not the ones standing in the front of the room. Understand what stage of their careers most of the members are in. Ideally, you'll want this to be equal or above your own. Rules, stated objectives, and purpose can all be read on a website or described by a current member. You can only evaluate the personality of the group and how it fits with your own by attending.

Use these five steps for choosing the right group and enjoy building relationships with others in a structured and supportive way. I attribute choosing groups like YPO to join as a significant part of my success as a professional. Remember too that groups are an optimal way to help support your personal and charitable goals. Nearly every hobby, charity, profession, or interest has a group to support it. Choose yours wisely and enjoy the benefits of relationship building and giving to others as you interact within the organization.

# Networking in Groups

The adage, *"it's not what you know but who you know"* should be updated to *"it's not who you know, but who knows you"*. Professional networking groups are a great resource for gaining new contacts and enhancing your connections. These are groups of entrepreneurs, businesspeople and professionals who regularly hold meetings to discuss business matters and to find ways to help each member. Group members benefit by making contact with individuals who can help by providing useful information or access to key individuals. Clearly, effective networking in groups can generate a steady stream of referrals and help your business grow.

I am currently involved in a business group that has a mission to be a board of advisors. We gather monthly, all from different industries, to share our experiences and points of view. It is a small group of ten members, six of whom have been together for many years. Three members of this group are my close friends and clients, generating approximately $75k in revenue annually. Together we are advocates for new opportunities. Would you consider investing four hours per month in a group like this?

**Get out of your comfort zone.** Most people spend too much unproductive time networking with friends and colleagues and have little to show for their efforts. It's an easy road to follow. And while it's important to cultivate relationships in your current networks, to grow your business you need to challenge yourself to make new contacts. Don't get trapped into thinking you are too busy at work to join a networking group. Everyone can make the time. There are groups with various levels of commitment and some that meet for breakfast, at lunch and after work.

**How to find the right group.** There are thousands of national, regional and local networking groups out there. Do your research and be choosy. Search for appropriate possible groups on the internet, in trade and professional publications, your local Chamber of Commerce or simply by talking to other professionals. Decide how much time you can commit to a networking group. Some groups meet once a week, other groups may meet once a month. Evaluate the group's expectations, members and rules. Some groups have attendance requirements and most groups have membership fees. Search for more than one group and if time and budget permit, join two to three groups to maximize your networking ability and results. Or, better yet....start your own group.

**Dive in.** Ask to be a guest at a meeting before deciding to join. Some groups are by invitation only and they accept no more than one person from each profession. If you know someone who is in a group ask for a referral to that group. Evaluate the group closely and have a real reason to get involved and understand how you might fit in the group versus your objectives. Once you've found the right group(s), develop relationships with all members. To do this it is critically important to meet and stay in touch - even between meetings. Once you've committed to a group, challenge yourself to get involved at a deeper level. Be a leader, not just a member. You can contact the organizers to see if there's something you can contribute to the group as a whole. Perhaps you can speak on your area of expertise, organize an event, or volunteer to help with registrations, etc.

**Listen and Learn.** Networking is not about how many business cards you can hand out and collect, it's an opportunity for you to learn about others' goals. Spend more time with a new contact posing questions and collecting information. People will be more open to talking about themselves if you ask specific questions about what they do, their challenges, accomplishments and goals. By listening carefully, you can make quick assessments as to whether they would have any interest in the solutions you provide that can help them. Remember, give first then you may receive.

**Give vs. Get.** Most people waste the few precious moments they have with new and existing contacts by focusing on themselves. The objective of networking is not to expound on your credentials. The focus of relationship building should be on *giving*. Instead of thinking only about what you can gain...or get...from a relationship, think about how you can give. Relationships develop rapidly when you give and people will remember you. What do you have that is worth giving? Demonstrate that you can be a resource to others with your professional expertise, external business connections, internal business connections, and community and family connections. Spread the wealth - look for ways to *give* to all group members.

**Be a connector.** If you can't solve a problem, refer your new contacts to people in your network who can. The benefit of this approach is twofold. First, you'll be seen as a problem solver, and second, those people who benefit from your referrals are more likely to provide you with referrals in return.

**It takes time.** Don't expect to make connections that bring value to your business development efforts overnight. It takes time to develop meaningful relationships and mutual trust. Cultivate your new relationships by sending your email newsletter (with permission) or offering an invitation for coffee or a lunch date. There's no need to invest a lot of time developing your new relationships, it's more important to develop a continuous stream of contact. And remember to give first. If you can bring two connections together - great! If you can share an article or some other pertinent information - pass it along. It's about the number of "touches." Give it at least a year to really see results from your involvement in networking groups.

**Be productive.** There are many effective ways to network in groups, some far more productive than the typical personal conversation.

- Have a great "elevator speech" - a 30-second description that introduces you and the problems you solve.
- Knowing how to start a conversation is an essential networking tool. Be prepared to ask questions, give a compliment or tell a story.
- Use questions to identify an individual's primary concerns and at least one piece of personal information.

- Be sure to make notes about the people you meet - you can use the back of their business card. With so many new faces in a group, it can be easy to get confused. Each person feels important when you remember them.

**Follow up.** Almost more important than getting out there and networking is taking a little time to follow up. Your networking efforts will be a waste of time without effective data management. When you meet or contact people, enter the information you learn into your database or contact management system. Make note of their interests, what you've shared with them, and when and how to contact them next. People have short memories. Follow-up regularly with group members or they may forget you exist and more importantly they'll forget that you are the best person to solve their problem.

**Challenge yourself.** It's time to make a move. Get out there this month and start researching networking groups in your area. Make a goal to join or get referred to at least two groups this month. A small commitment of a few hours each month can really improve your visibility and change the way you do business. Heck, just for starters, join the Rotary Club - good for both you and the community.

# Your 30-Second Introduction

We live in a time where advertisement length attention spans are the norm. Learning to capture those short attention spans is crucial to success while relationship building in events and groups. We can easily capture someone's attention with a brief and powerful "self-introduction."

Have you ever attended an event where the facilitator asks for each person to keep their introduction brief, to around 30-seconds? Then, before long, someone monopolizes four precious minutes of an already tight agenda with "all about me" time at everyone else's expense. Others will follow suit, thinking that since they had to endure the first lengthy-diatribe it is their due.

I used to think this happened do to insensitive or self-centered personalities who simply couldn't be bothered to respect other people time enough to follow direction. After years of training and coaching others, I now know that most people rave and ramble when they introduce themselves because they simply do not understand how to structure a powerful and succinct self-introduction.

We already know that most people are not comfortable with public speaking and even fewer are good at short-format impromptu speaking, so it is necessary for most of us to take the time to practice keeping our introductions short and sweet. We want to do this because these first short impressions create a lasting legacy. Less is more. Clutter can destroy others ability to understand who you are and what you do.

Being succinct shows respect for other's time and enables you to establish rapport and move on to asking great questions. We've all seen it at events, the person who stands up and grabs the room's attention with an eloquent and interesting self-introduction. Follow these techniques and that person will be you.

## How to craft a 30-second introduction:

1. Give your name and describe the benefit of what you do in a few words. It is much more compelling to say, "Hi my name is Amber, and I help people see their toes," then to say, "Hi my name is Amber, and I'm a nutritionist."

2. Share a recent customer success or a key piece of one of your passions in just a sentence. A great example is, "Recently I was able to help a client lose 45 lbs in four months without dieting, but by making a lifestyle change." Or, "I love the way it feels to meditate on the open road when I ride my motorcycle." Keep it short, sweet and original.

3. Share your objectives based on the success or passion you shared. Now that you've told how you help others and given an example, it's time to ask for what you want. Be specific and brief. Your request should be appropriate to where you are with the group. As a new member of an organization, you might be asking to have a conversation. In a group you've belonged to for a long time you might look for a specific referral or type of support. For instance, "If you work with women in their 40's or 50's I would love to get to know you better."

4. Close with a powerful statement or tagline. Every major brand has a tagline because these simple memory-jarring phrases help anchor you in the minds of others. When interacting in new groups and introducing yourself to many at one time it is a good idea to use one to leave a dramatic impact. When talking to an individual, ending your introduction with a tagline can sound canned and inauthentic. Instead, use a powerful statement about something you are passionate about. For example, I

usually share my passion for helping others get what they want at the end of my introduction because it creates interest and encourages questions.

Create your own 30-second introductions and grab the short attention spans before they pass you by. Take time to practice and to create several introductions to fit the varying situations in your life. You will never be caught with nothing to say again!

# Successfully Networking at Events

Every year I attend trade shows, conferences, and other events to learn, to network, and to broaden my understanding of my business practices. While there, I enjoy catching up with colleagues, the interaction with other attendees at break-out sessions, listening to the keynote speaker, and it seems I always take away something valuable. My goal is to take away at least one new idea, one new contact and one new product solution for our clients. While a day or two away from my normal routine can be a welcome break, I always reflect on what I will really gain before accepting an invitation or sending in my registration. I have also discovered that a little time spent on preparation prior to going to a meeting makes a big difference in how successful the event is for me.

## Planning.

I receive numerous invitations to industry, motivational and innovation events each year. When deciding if and which to attend, I consider multiple facets of the event prior to commitment.

First, most events have certain groups of people that bring something of value to the table. Who is on the guest list? Who are the attendees? I try to find out who will be there and identify if there are people or representatives from companies who can help implement personal and business strategies for growth.

Then I look to see the type of venue and the schedule of events. Will this venue house all the attendees? Will it be conducive to meet other people? Are there enough surrounding offsite meeting spots to find places for one-on-one meetings if needed? If the opportunity exists to schedule a meeting with someone who will be attending the same event, I always do so ahead of time. I view the hotel as an extension of the event and if the program is out of town, I stay at the "right" hotel.

Lastly, I look at the resources for their content and availability prior and post sessions as some resources are for hire and some are only on a speaking circuit. I call the speaker circuit group, "information dumpers." Have you ever gone up to meet a speaker after a talk, wait patiently in a line, only to find out the resource is a paid speaker and does not make house calls? These people are motivational and only to be heard from again at the next big gathering. Seeking out resources that can help implement strategy and develop my business is one of the keys to event participation.

**Purpose.**
Quite possibly the most important step in the process of attending the right event is to identify my purpose in attending. I may be more interested in meeting someone or I might attend primarily due to the nature of the event. When my focus is on making connections, my mindset is very different than if I am there to gather information for the growth of a technical aspect of my business, or something I should be learning to enhance my personal and family life. Of course, sometimes I attend an event with multiple purposes. In these cases, I take a close look at the agenda and plan my day around the most important sessions while leaving ample time to meet new and interesting people. Meeting new people at the event can be just by coincidence, haphazard or planned. All three are to be expected and worthy of note. The fact that we are getting out in the world sharing our point of view and being available for approach is a key factor of its success. Admittedly, sometimes I just show up and wing it - we all do this on occasion. However, I have the most success when I am focused on my connection to the event, the resources and the attendees.

Some events are part of my "hood". I enjoy planning and being part of meetings where I have input. At least one time a year I am part of a planning committee, an event organizer and/or a member of a board sponsoring an event. In these cases, I usually provide input throughout the year to help design the event and project its outcome. Being connected in this fashion provides a huge opportunity for growth in every aspect of personal and business development. My role and relationship to the organization is key in making meaningful, lifelong connections.

**Post-Event.**
After an event I reflect on the people I have met, go through the business cards I collected and carefully think through...*did I make any meaningful connections? Did I develop deeper relationships with existing contacts?* I carefully go through the business cards I collected, try to put a face to each one and associate a conversation. I am realistic, as I do discard many, knowing that a future connection may not lead either party in a direction for growth. Those that I keep, I make notes on to spark my memory - things that stick out in my mind about the person, their business, or our possible connection. I always add them to my database and follow up with a quick email or phone call to set a date for coffee or lunch.

Successful networking at events takes some forethought and planning. With practice, you will discover how to make connections that will lead to personal and professional growth.

# How to Overcome Networking Hurdles

Over the course of your lifetime, networking will be the single most effective strategy used in advancing your career, developing your business and enhancing your life. Learning the skills for effective networking is worth the time and energy it requires. While we can all benefit immensely by learning networking techniques and practices, we are often confronted by hurdles that prevent us from being truly effective.

## Hurdle #1: Uncomfortable Meeting New People.

- **Focus on "them".** It's not about you and it's all about them. By taking the emphasis off you and your performance, you reduce the pressure and have set yourself up for success. When your focus is on another, it is harder to become self-conscious, boastful, or say something you'd regret.

- **Dress for success.** Like it or not, most of another person's perception of you is based on how you look. If you're in doubt about how to dress, it's best to err on the side of conservatism. It is much better to be overdressed than underdressed. If you're not sure, check with the person organizing the event and ask. When you are dressed appropriately, you will have more confidence.

- **Get referred.** Ask for an introduction. People like to be "connectors". It makes them feel important to know that they have connected two people with similar interests. Just like when you have an opportunity to recommend your favorite restaurant to someone... it makes you feel good to share this information.

- **Follow passions.** It's easy to network while you are doing what you like to do. Think about your hobbies and recreational activities. It is cliché, but we all know that a lot of business (and networking) is done on the golf course. But what else do you do for fun? You can always meet people at the gym, football game, tennis match, art class, etc. Don't take off your networking cap on the weekend!

- **Pick "softer" targets.** Very often we aim too high for comfort. For example you may want to meet the CEO of a company. Going direct on a business angle may not yield the results. Try to find a way to meet through a charity, community activity or children. People see us through different lenses that often create unexpected opportunities.

## Hurdle # 2: Unable to Find the Time.

- **Be aware.** Use every opportunity, every day, everywhere because networking can take place at any time. Organized networking events are obvious places to make connections, but high school and family reunions, weddings, graduations, bar mitzvahs and even (when appropriate) funerals can offer opportunities to meet and connect with new people.

- **Never eat alone.** Breakfast and lunch are perfect for networking. If time is at a premium (and for most of us, it is), be sure to schedule meetings (one-on-one or small groups) in the morning for breakfast and at lunch. Not only will you find an extra hour or two in your day, but your connections may also appreciate the thought... and the extra time they will find in their day!

- **Use technology.** It may take some time, but the learning curve for social networking is not a steep one. Social networking is an inexpensive means for connecting with others, enhancing your presence, and positioning yourself as an expert in your field. It's probably safe to say that LinkedIn has more professional users than any other site and has the greatest number of searchable and reachable executives and corporate decision makers than any other social media venue. You might also consider Twitter, Facebook, Foursquare, etc. Email marketing is another way to reach people using technology. There are several companies out there that can help with customized templates, list management and other invaluable tools to connect electronically with others. Remember that your company or business may restrict or prevent the use of certain social media outlets, so check out the rules first.

- **Prioritize.** Any busy person who discovered a new passion or a fun new hobby has found that it is possible to find the time when you strongly want to do something. Suddenly, your schedule opens up, you find new efficiencies, or you are able to reprioritize. If you're not able to do that with networking, revisit your beliefs and your purpose.

- **Internal opportunities.** Many opportunities actually exist during your normal schedule. The people you work with on a daily basis may be connectors as they can often refer you to people that you should be connected to. Raise your profile and move up the ladder. There may be internal networking opportunities within your own firm. Put yourself out there and try to meet the principles of your firm. By positioning yourself as someone who is interested in business development for yourself and the firm, you may be remembered and recognized for promotion when the time comes.

## Hurdle #3: Don't Know What to Say.

- **You are interesting.** Do you feel like you can't be a good networking because you are an introvert? Or do feelings of shyness hold you back from networking? These feelings contribute to the misconception that only outgoing people are good at networking. Having no clear purpose and needing to work on our social skills can compound feelings of shyness, which are basically a lack of self-confidence. Preparation and planning can create confidence, which causes us to be successful which make us more confident

- **Conversation boosters.** Whether networking one-on-one or in a group, it's good to have some conversations ready to go. People like to talk about their vacation, the best job they ever had, the one thing they could change about their work/career. Technology is also a good conversation starter. It's all around us: "I see you have an iPhone, what is your favorite gadget"? Learning to be a good story teller is a great way to keep the conversation going. Practice your "go to" story ahead of time. Pick a topic of interest, keep it short, and make sure it's clear and has a message. Stories should be positive, enthusiastic and not mention any names (individuals or companies), unless appropriate.

- **Ask questions.** Be curious. People like to talk about themselves and their successes. Whether it's work achievements, their family, or sports triumphs, most people relish the opportunity to brag a bit. Let them.... no, encourage them!

- **Be complimentary.** Don't be shy in paying someone a compliment. For example, "I like your tie" or "I love your watch." This does not have to appear to brown-nosing or trying to win points. Open and honest compliments are part of a normal daily experience. Use it!

- **Listen.** Networking is more about listening than talking. While most of us are too consumed with *what am I going to say* we are not as worried about being unable to listen. Listening to someone is a form of flattery.

## Hurdle #4: Lack of a Plan.

- **Define your goals.** There are ways to be much more efficient and effective with the time you spend networking. Instead of very general events with a random groups of people, take time to research exactly whom you need to add to your network and target your networking time accordingly. You may even want to create your own networking events and activities. This would be a larger investment of time, but the return is much greater when you are the organizer and host. There are also networking events that are better suited for a more introverted person. Large, non-agenda meetings can be difficult for anyone if you are unfamiliar with the group. Focus on smaller, more personal events to build your confidence.

- **Do your homework.** Find out ahead of time who will be attending the event and identify who you would like to meet. What is the agenda? Are there sessions you should attend and can you carve out some time in between for the sole purpose of meeting people? If you can, try to schedule time with people prior to the event. Who are the key sponsors? Are there any reciprocal opportunities or reasons to meet the sponsors that may help your business?

**Hurdle #5: Don't Like to Sell.**

- **It isn't selling.** May I have your attention please? NETWORKING IS NOT SELLING!

- **Give vs. Get.** The focus of networking should be mainly on giving. Instead of thinking only about what you can gain...or get...from a relationship, think about how you can give. Relationships develop rapidly when you give and people will remember you. What do you have that is worth giving? Demonstrate that you can be a resource to others with your professional expertise, external business connections, internal business connections, and community and family connections.

- **Understand needs.** Spending time with someone with whom you will eventually have a long term relationship requires a keen ear and acute listening skills. Once we understand someone's desires and personal makeup we can truly help them through possible network and personal connections.

- **Identify who can help.** We all have our own unique and individual network of friends, family and associates. Very often we uncover something for a friend, family member or associate that needs attention. For example, you may hear someone's mom has a particular illness and is looking for a specialist - you may know someone who can help either directly or through an introduction.

## Hurdle #6. Society's Obstacles

- **Don't talk to strangers.** As children, we were all taught that we shouldn't talk to (or take candy from) a stranger. Get this out of your head! While meeting new people doesn't appear difficult, it rarely feels that way. Anxieties, social politeness and an unwillingness to get rejected may keep you from taking the first step. These hurdles are really just excuses. There are rules we keep inside our head of when it is and isn't appropriate to meet people. While some of these rules have some basis in reality, most of them are wrong.

Overcoming hurdles is about courage. Getting out in a big way requires a little faith and a willingness to take some risks. Think carefully about your excuses for avoiding networking in relation to these six common obstacles. Nearly every one of them is founded in the way we think. Once we've removed these obstacles that come between ourselves and our goal of effective networking, our success is assured. Apply diligence to make sure you're not allowing bad thinking habits and doubt to creep back in. From now on, it's simply a matter of time and consistent effort.

# Networking Event Code

Wikipedia defines **code of conduct** as *"a set of rules outlining the responsibilities of or proper practices for an individual, party or organization."* In the many years I have attended, organized, sponsored, and spoken at various events, there seems to be an unofficial, unspoken "Event Code" that has nothing to do with rules and is more about proper practices and etiquette in relation to conversation, body language, and behavior.

The first, and maybe most difficult, step in networking is joining and starting conversations. To be a successful networker, you must learn to join a conversation, or you should just stay home. Try a less intimidating approach first; make eye contact, smile and approach someone standing alone. Once you are comfortable approaching a single person, join a group already in conversation. Identify a small group and gently tap someone on the arm, say hello and shake hands. Whenever you join a group, smile and nod, be polite and don't speak until acknowledged. Also don't expect a round of introductions.

My approach has always been to be prepared with some conversation starters. These may include sharing your dream vacation or the best job/assignment/client you ever had. You may feel comfortable offering up one thing you would change about your work or career and then ask someone in the group what they might change. Technology is around us all the time and is a great way to prompt a conversation about a new phone or gadget.

Three components to successful event interaction are words, tone and body language. The words we choose to use and how we use them are part of our personal brand. Choosing words carefully while being polite and avoiding insult is most important. Speaking tone should be authoritative and friendly. If you have a compelling message and authentic passion about something, it will come through in your tone of voice. Awareness of these branding components when speaking with new people will make a world of difference; remember what they say about first impressions…

When you become more comfortable networking, you may begin to develop some storytelling skills. Your stories should be enthusiastic and positive - you don't want new connections to remember you as being depressing or sad. Your stories should avoid complaining and should be anonymous; never specifically mentioning names unless appropriate. When telling a story, keep it short with a clear message. Practice a few of your favorite stories and be prepared to try them out at your next event.

Nobody can say for certain exactly how much body language influences a first impression, but it clearly has a tremendous impact on relationship development. You will put people at ease if you are engaged and interested in what they have to say - this is recognized when you smile and nod "yes" while listening. Avoid "room grazing" - make eye contact with the speaker. You should also stand square-shouldered or lean forward, if seated. Remember the episode of Seinfeld where Kramer is put off guard by Elaine's new boyfriend, the "close talker"? Or how about another episode when Jerry has a huge misunderstanding with a woman who was a "soft talker?" The rule of thumb for personal space in a conversation is 3 feet, or an arm's length. And if you are a quiet talker….speak up and be heard!

Networking at an event is about making new connections and driving deeper relationships with existing connections. Set yourself a networking goal ahead of time. Plan to meet five new people and make a point to remain in a conversation no longer than five minutes. As engaging as a conversation may be, eventually it is time to move on - gracefully and politely. How? Be honest. Explain that your goal is to meet five people today and that you would like to move on. Before you do so, however, sum up the conversation, exchange business cards, and make a tentative plan to follow-up with a phone call, an email, a date for coffee, etc. Then, make eye contact, shake hands and move along.

When is the appropriate time to follow-up after a networking event? RIGHT AWAY! The next day is the perfect time to send a quick email. Remind the person that you met at a certain event, say how you enjoyed meeting the person, and the reasons why you two should connect. Then be sure to review the business cards you collected, make notes, and add the contacts to your database.

So while Wikipedia may not have a definition for Event Code there are some unspoken practices for networking events. The bottom line is that to be successful at networking events, it takes some practice and experience and of course, good manners.

## Connect and Thrive

All the various parts of our life create opportunities to be part of different networks and to move among them all the time. For instance, you might be a part of a sports team, a theater company, a Rotary Club, a BNI Group, a PTA or any of the thousands of other groups of people coming together with a common interest. How you view the different groups you socialize with whether in life or your business, matters a great deal. All the people that we know do not necessarily know each other–in fact it makes it easier to be a connector if they don't–all the people that we know have one thing in common: they know you.

Think about it this way, we are the center of a wheel with many spokes; at each end of the spoke is another sphere. Each of these spheres has connection too! The opportunity to connect is exponential. The only stumbling blocks, ourselves. So how and why do we bring our outlying spheres together?

The why is simple. We are on a journey to positively affect the lives of as many people we know. After all, it is our life experience we share. The how is a step-by-step approach to changing our habits.

One of my habits is to have a breakfast meeting every day. Sometimes I even have two. I can meet someone for eggs and coffee at 7:30 and another person at 9:00. By the time most people are finishing their first cup of coffee, I have two meetings under my belt. I hear this all the time, "I don't have time to do this." What I do is sleep a little less. Sleep is overrated.

My own relationships are diverse and separate based on the various brands that make me Andrew Bluestone—trainer, salesman, author, father, motorcycle enthusiast, nonprofit affiliate—all different brands with different networks. All these people, groups and events have one common denominator is me—Andrew Bluestone.

I have the chance to make a difference in many lives by connecting those who need each other in some way. I can contribute to the individuals in my network through the power of introduction or referral. If my neighbor needs a new roof, I could introduce him to the roofer in my Rotary group. In this way, I am making connections between my networks and giving back.

Personal connectors are very well known in their communities. Connectors are respected. Paul Revere was a connector. That is why history remembers him. He didn't have the loudest voice, and he was not the leading figure in the American Revolution, but everyone knows who he was.

Becoming a connector is easy, but it requires practice. We all have many different groups of which we are naturally a part. Luckily, these groups often come together for special events such as weddings, birthdays, and community work. This is a great place to make introductions and co-mingle your different groups of friends and colleagues.

# Create a Networking Event

Organizing your own networking event is a smart way to establish yourself as a leader and the center of an expanding network. Let's look into how and why it is so effective: 1) you will take charge of expanding your network while becoming a connector, 2) you create a reason for people to want to know you and to be a part of your network, 3) it will strengthen your own relationships, and 4) you can genuinely help other people. Creating a networking event should not be for the sole purpose of recruiting new customers from the group – rather, you'll want to build trust and give people the space to get to know each other.

**Type of event.** There are several different types of events. Host a program with a speaker sharing content that is timely and pertinent, where attendees are gathered in a seminar or conference room. Create an environment where people would take turns going around the circle, explaining what they do and what kind of new clients they would and can develop. Or you might envision a large group gathering, with freestyle networking and a massive exchange of business cards. Perhaps a speed networking event is more your style. Your event may include a light breakfast or it may be an after work cocktail event. Inviting a guest speaker with an agenda or pre-established program on a particular topic will attract a base of longtime event participants. Whether you are considering regular monthly gatherings or a one-time event, any of these types of networking events can be highly successful.

**Target audience.** Although it's simple to say that your invitation list should be people with similar interests, the common denominator may really only be that you are inviting a group of people interested in business development. Invite people who are looking to improve skills and those around them. Attendees from a broad range of industries may present a greater business opportunity to you or others.

**Venue logistics.** Your event should be easy to get to and to find. Easy access to highways and public transportation is as important as convenient parking. If attendees will be travelling from out of town, nearby affordable overnight accommodations should be available. The room should be large enough for your group with ample room for refreshments and mingling.

**How long.** Depending on the type of event you are hosting, the duration will vary. Typically a networking event with a speaker and time for mingling after will be one to two hours whether the time of day is breakfast, lunch or an after work cocktail.

**Financial arrangements.** There may be considerable cost associated with hosting event. You should plan accordingly and decide if you will charge a fee to attend. If so, you will need to have a procedure in place for registering and paying the fee. Perhaps you have or can establish the ability to accept credit cards via PayPal. Another approach is to find sponsors who can share the expenses associated with hosting your event.

**Sponsors.** Sponsors can share in the cost of hosting an event. A sponsor can simply promote his or her services in exchange for monetary involvement, or may contribute to the event by participating and adding value to the content of the program. Find a niche and within that niche you will find there are plenty of sponsorship opportunities.

**Marketing.** Don't forget to promote the event. Rule of thumb is that you should "start the buzz" 5-6 weeks prior. Do this by word of mouth, posting on social media, including it in your newsletters or by sending save the date cards or emails. Then, 3-4 weeks before the event, make an official announcement by sending out the invitations, posting on social media, websites, email campaigns, etc.

**Follow up.** Ask each attendee to sign in or collect business cards by putting out a fish bowl for a door prize drawing. As with any event you might otherwise attend, don't forget to follow up with new contacts by sending an email note or making a phone call to connect one on one for coffee or lunch. Also, you've put a lot of effort in the planning and execution of this event. Leverage the effort! Think about doing it again in another location. Have the next meeting in queue and announce it at this event….with another group of invitees, and/or with another agenda.

**Advantages.** By hosting your own networking event you can tailor it exactly the way you want. You can limit the number of participants, you can invite only certain people in certain industries…you basically control every aspect. You also position yourself as an expert, a resource and a connector.

**Cautions.** Hosting an event takes a lot of time and real commitment. Remember, your name is on the door! Whether things go really well or very badly, the event is a reflection on you.

# How to Organize a Networking Event

When I want to expand my network, organizing my own networking event is a great way to make new connections. There are many types of networking events, ranging from small groups with a targeted focus to large groups where hundreds attend to hear keynote speakers, partake in a meal and have an opportunity to do some freestyle networking. The types of events that I prefer to host are "medium sized" events - 20 to 50 attendees. The take home value in my events is always some information that is timely, pertinent, or is of general interest to the group. The content is either provided by me or by someone that I have chosen to partner with for the event.

Depending on the size and scope or your event, there are variables to consider before, during and after the event. My events are fairly simple to organize, and I use an action plan similar to below:

## Before the Event:
- Select and confirm a partner, co-host or presenter. The benefits of partnering with someone is that it broadens the range of information you may want to present and it extends your invitation list to networks beyond your own.
- Meet with partners to determine program content and start working on hand-outs, if any. Print appropriate quantities of program materials and your company's promotional materials.

- Set a date and time. Usually Mondays and Fridays should be avoided, as well as the day before or after a holiday. Depending on your invitees, you may also need to avoid quarter-end or year-end. Decide if the event should be in the morning, during the day or after work.
- Create a guest list. Sometimes I focus my events on a particular industry or group, or I may open it up to a range of people across various professions and industries. This is also a good time to decide if invitees should be encouraged to bring a friend/colleague, or not. The success of your event will rest largely on the quality of the attendees, so make your guest list carefully.
- Select and reserve a facility. It could be at your office, a local restaurant or club, a library meeting room, a community center, etc. Ensure the venue is easy to find and has adequate parking.
- Determine your budget and decide if you will charge a fee to cover expenses such as venue rental, refreshments, materials, etc.
- Five to six weeks before the event, I try to start some "buzz" by announcing the upcoming event on my website, in my email newsletters and on LinkedIn. You might also want to post to any other social media networks you use. Of course, I always talk it up when I see and talk to people. Also consider sending a "save the date" email or postcard five to six weeks prior.
- Invite guests three to four weeks before the event. I use an email marketing service that also offers event marketing and online registration. My contacts are uploaded to this service, then I create an invitation, a registration page, an event webpage and if needed, set-up the ability to receive payments.
- My company has the ability to offer CE credits for accountants at certain events. When certifications are offered, they should be printed and signed and made available for attendees on the day of the event.
- Print name tags (double-check spelling). Since this is a networking event and you want to facilitate conversation, ask everyone to put a fun fact on their name tags when they arrive.

- Provide some kind of food or drinks. Contact caterer or local coffee shop to discuss cost, amount and type of refreshments, keeping in mind the time of day and duration of your event.
- Order signs, balloons, etc. to brand your event and to promote your business.

**During the Event:**
- Arrive early to set up. Make sure there are enough seats and materials for all attendees.
- Provide a sign-in sheet or other method to capture contact information, i.e. name, company, phone number, email address.
- Meet and greet your guests. Relax, smile and be as personable as possible.
- Begin and end the meeting on time.
- When the event begins, welcome everyone and introduce those who don't know each other or have each person introduce themselves. And don't forget to talk about yourself and what you're looking for. The control you have on this event is how you solidify your role as the center of this network.
- As the host, focus on spending time to connect with new opportunities. If you have guests you already know, find a time to speak/meet with them outside the event to optimize your time there.
- Collect business cards, and be sure to write notes for following up later- you won't remember everything. Plus, it makes people feel important when you write down what they say.
- Facilitate mingling by warmly and gently approaching those who appear a bit "lost" and striking up a conversation. Ask questions about what they do and what kind of characteristics their ideal client would possess, and introduce them to another nearby person (even if you don't know that person and have to introduce yourself at the same time). Then you can leave these two new connected individuals together so you can repeat the process elsewhere if needed.
- Promote yourself. Just because you've coordinated the event, it doesn't mean you should avoid promoting yourself.

- Use a takeaway to make it easy for your guest to remember you. The takeaway can be a branded gift like a pen, water bottle, umbrella, or simply programs materials.

## After the Event:
- Thank everyone for their time within a week after the event. There are a couple of ways to do this:
    - If you are forming a group and more events will follow, sending a group email is a great way to bring the group together and provide email addresses to all.
    - Write a blog post, a website update, or post on LinkedIn or Facebook to summarize the event and thank attendees (this is also a great way to create interest in future events).
    - Send a personal email to each attendee - a simple thank you or a request to follow up with your best opportunities over breakfast or lunch.
- Follow up with any leads or connections you made. Add your prospects to your database or contact management system. Make note of their interests, what you've shared with them, and when and how to contact them next. Call your leads and tell them you enjoyed meeting them. Find ways you can help each other's business. Send referrals and ask for referrals. Be specific about what you need.
- Get feedback. Conduct a survey after the event and see how you could improve for next time.
- Pay any bills - catering, rentals, printing, etc.
- Start planning your next event!

Your event is *your* opportunity to make new business acquaintances and influence people. Now that it's all planned, enjoy the networking!

# Section 4 —
# Maintaining and Organizing Contacts

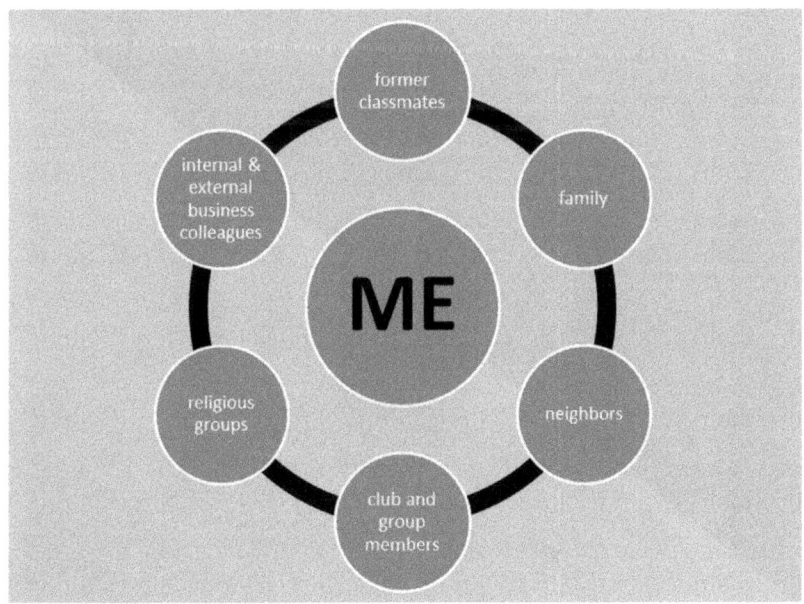

# Be a Generator. Learn to Hunt.

Every organization includes two types of producers: advisors and associates – Hunters and Gatherers.

Hunters represent approximately 20 percent of advisors and associates, but consistently produce 80 percent of the new business in a firm! Why is that? Well, if you study the hunters' habits and traits, you'll discover they have seven characteristics in common.

It all starts with your network and your ability to build the trusting relationships that may help generate positive, rewarding results. Study the hunter, adopt the hunter's behaviors and become a generator!

- **Hunters are prepared.** They invest time in uncovering prospects and bring the right ideas to the meeting. They believe achievements are the result of preparation.
- **Hunters are relationship builders.** They know that all things being equal, prospects buy from the sales rep they know, trust and like. More importantly, they understand that all things NOT being equal, buyers do the same thing -- they buy from sales reps they know, trust and like.
- **Hunters work at the right things.** They focus on those few sales activities that are attainable and make a clear difference in the lives they touch.
- **Hunters always have a sales call objective.** Intention creates a "bottom line result" as they enter every selling situation.

- **Hunters ask probing questions.** They ask the right questions -- the questions that arouse interest with prospects. They develop questions that uncover strategies and needs that generate a desire to purchase.
- **Hunters talk to the decision makers.** They deliver the message to the appropriate decision maker. They do not want to give their presentation for practice.
- **Hunters manage the buying process.** They present strategies that move the prospect to a decision to buy.

# The Power of the Unnecessary Letter

The power is right at your fingertips...literally.

When was the last time you took the time to write a handwritten thank you note? I do this regularly. Once I realized its power in terms of relationship building, I became committed to this form of communication. I've made a habit of sending handwritten thank you notes and believe it is a vital strategy in both my business and personal lives.

Recently I sent a note to my friend JoJo who has been the tailgate party host at MetLife Stadium (formerly Giant's Stadium) for the past twelve years. His tailgate party starts hours before the game begins and often continues right through the game itself as people prefer to watch the game on the portable television in the parking lot! We all appreciate the effort and thank our host at the end of each game. At the close of every football season, I also send a handwritten thank you note. It's short, succinct and complimentary. I don't expect anything in return. Never have and never will. It's a thank you note, a note of appreciation, a note from the heart. This year, after receiving my note, my friend called me. "You have always supported me and as much as you appreciate my tailgate parties, I just want *you* to know, without your attendance, support and good cheer, our tailgate parties would not be the same". With that he continued, "I have obtained a few tickets to the Super Bowl and would like you to come to my first tailgate party in Indianapolis" (the location of Super Bowl XLII.) We went to the Super Bowl. We set up a makeshift tailgate party, we all went into the stadium (no portable television for this event!), and had a great time!

## The Power of the Unnecessary Letter

Did I need to send this note? Was it unnecessary? Maybe. But the fact is that it made me stand out. Sure, a verbal thank you is nice and the very *least* that's required when someone goes the extra mile to provide support to an individual, an organization, or a goal. An emailed thank you is okay, but it doesn't stick past the moment the "delete" key is hit. When I receive a thank you card in the mail it shows me that my contribution was noticed and that the person or organization that sent it to me is grateful for my efforts. It also makes me much more likely to give generously again. Go old school with your thanks. In this high tech world of emails and text messages the simple and quick act of writing a handwritten expression of gratitude can go a long way. There's something special today about a handwritten note and it should only take about three minutes per card.

You may at first feel uncomfortable about writing a thank you note or unsure about what to say. There is a seven-point formula for writing the proper thank-you. Try it out, master it, and it will become habit and more rewarding before you know it.

Greet the giver. That's the easy part, but you'd be surprised by how many people forget it. Use what makes you comfortable: *Dear Joe, Hi Mary, Hello David*. Dale Carnegie taught us people love to hear their own names and direct marketing has proven that we also love to read them in print.

Be specific. Start off by saying "Thank you," then directly state exactly what you are thankful for.

Express your gratitude. Be clear, specific and sincere in why you are appreciative. Avoid vague statements like "I appreciate what you did. Thanks a lot." Say something nice about the gift or the act that you are grateful for.

Mention the past, allude to the future. "It was great to see you at the networking event; I hope to see you at next month's meeting."

It's about them, not you. What shouldn't be included in your note is news about your life, bragging about a new job, or anything else that's not focused on the recipient.

Wrap it up. Again, use whatever closing works for you: *Regards, Sincerely, Best*.

Sign it. Your signature should be neat and identifiable, not your autograph scrawl. Then neatly address the envelope, stamp it and get it in the mail.

There may be only one day a year devoted to giving thanks, but expressing thanks regularly - year round - and doing it well is one of the most profitable business strategies you can have. We know that relationship building is dependent upon making connections, but it's also about building enduring, mutually beneficial relationships. The habit of sending a short note of thanks gives you the power to keep the communication loop open between you and another person.

> *"Appreciative words are the most powerful force for good on earth."*
> —George W. Crane

# The Art of Email Introductions

A great way to strengthen your network is to introduce two people who could benefit from knowing each other. When you introduce two people, you have the advantage of familiarity with both parties. The advantage is in your sincere commitment to help two strangers learn something about one another. Since both people are busy make it easy for them to take action and quickly decide if knowing each other makes sense.

The most common type of introduction is emailing each person simultaneously. In this way, you make the connection while making it clear WHY the two individuals should meet. Here's what an email introduction might look like:

## The Art of Email Introductions

> From: Andy
> To: Joe Smith, Mary Jones
> Subject: Introduction
>
> Joe, I want to introduce you to Mary Jones. Mary has been a friend of mine since college. She is a partner at XYZ Partners. Her forensic accounting work has helped her clients uncover bookkeeping mistakes and solve liquidity issues.
>
> Mary, Joe is a successful entrepreneur and former business partner. He is looking for resources to help him in his new business endeavors.
>
> I hope you two will connect with each other.
>
> Regards,
> Andy

Now let us suppose you are on the RECEIVING end of an email introduction. Here's how to reply:

Click Reply All but move the introducer to the Cc line. If I've taken the time to introduce two people, I want to know that they've actually taken the next step to connect, but do not need or want to be copied on all the future back-and-forth emails.

Thank the introducer for making the introduction.

Introduce yourself to the other person and go from there.

Here's a sample reply:

> *From: Mary Jones*
> *To: Joe Smith*
> *cc: Andy*
> *Subject: Introduction*
>
> *Thanks for the intro, Andy.*
>
> *Nice to meet you, Joe. I would love to line up a chat to get acquainted and to share what I've been doing at XYZ Partners. In short, we do forensic accounting with a focus on start-ups. Definitely think that there are some ways we can be helpful to each other.*
>
> *Do you have some time this week to chat via phone or meet up for coffee? Here are a few days/times that work for a call:*
> *Mon May 23 - 2pm to 3:30pm EST*
> *Wed May 25 - 2pm to 6pm EST*
> *Thu May 26 - 11am to 2pm EST*
>
> *Hope to talk soon.*
> *Mary*

**Tips to remember:**

- Make it personal. A personal connection makes it more likely he/she will trust the other person and respond to maintain the friendship with you.
- Be specific about who each connection is and how you are connected to each of them.
- Briefly highlight each of their achievements.
- Demonstrate commonality or how you think that each might be of use to the other as a connection.

# The Art of Email Introductions

- Less is more. Boil it down into as few sentences as possible while still conveying the message you want received.
- Clearly say why you're connecting both parties to each other.
- It must be individual. You should only try to connect two people at a time. If you attempt to create several new connections in one email it becomes confusing.
- When responding to an introduction, be sure to move the introducer to the Cc line so he/she can see that the connection was made and is taken out of the loop of follow-on correspondence.
- Include a sentence at the end telling the two people you've just introduced that it's up to them to take it further.

## The Power of Intention

Relationships develop and deepen over time. This leads to other contacts and opportunities.

We are gregarious in nature. We create relationships in the course of everyday life. Honoring our natural desire to connect and develop camaraderie is a choice. We can fulfill that end through networking if we approach it with purpose.

Building, maintaining, and growing a strong support group takes time and dedication too. When you give someone support, encouragement, or a recommendation, your network is bound to grow. It is easy to lose track of exactly what we are giving and receiving. That's the point. We don't keep score.

When I think about the evolution of relationships, and how it must be nurtured, I am reminded of a long-term influential client of mine in New Jersey. We've worked together for over twelve years.

Each year we develop more trust and confidence in each other and the relationship becomes more rewarding as a result.

I first met this gentleman in 2001. We ran in a few of the same circles, and I knew he would be a fixture in my life. I knew this relationship would be important, because we could help each other achieve like-minded goals.

Early on in our relationship I asked, "What can I do to help you?"

One simple and powerful question led to an early connection which has fulfilled both of our personal and business aspirations. We are not only able to connect on a business level. We connect socially as well—on golf outings, sporting events, and family vacations.

As we spend more social time together our business relationship also strengthens. Does that make sense? You bet it does!

So simple. So comfortable. Why don't we do this all the time?

The first year I worked with him on a few deals to help each other. One of which, was a tax-saving financial instrument that we implemented together. Then, my company was able to help with college savings plans. Over the next several years we would continue to work together to secure his financial future with long term care planning, life insurance, and a retirement program for his company. On the flipside, I supported him with introductions to my business and political relationships that supported his personal and business goals.

Every year our relationship deepens and becomes more fruitful for both of us. Through my ability to meet his family's needs, his trust in our relationship grew so strong that he honored me with the management of his company's 401(k) plan and began referring me to local government offices and other business owners to help manage their needs. Every year our relationship becomes stronger and yes, with the additional trust, our relationship becomes more financially lucrative as well.

All the rewards happened because I began a relationship with intention—with the commitment to his success which quickly became a reciprocal commitment to mine.

The likelihood of success through relationship development greatly increases with time. The longer you know someone, with a consistent commitment to helping them through your connections, the stronger the relationship will become.

Business development requires conscious action along with a clear plan. It doesn't happen by accident. As a way of life, networking incorporates attitude, awareness, and action. You can be very aware of people and opportunities, and yet it is only when you take action to bring those people together that results occur.

You are the center and source of your network. You have available to you a multitude of resources to trade, share, and pass along to others. Being a resource means that you are proactive about looking for ways to pass along what you know. People may not always take you up on your offers. The information or contacts that you have may not always turn out the way you hoped. No matter. The act of helping and offering generates good will.

# Choosing the *Right* Relationships

Adding new people to your network is exciting. It is necessary to remember that you could meet thousands of people a day and it would all be for naught if you don't keep track of them in some way.

Although we may want to keep a database of everyone we meet, we can't build strong relationships with everyone. Choosing the *right* network will help you be more comfortable and more successful.

Who should you be in relationships with?

There are three distinct groups of people you will be building into your network—professional targets, family and friends, and community connections. When you think about your network in this way it might surprise you how many people you already know. In fact, in my experience most of us have at least one thousand people in our network already!

Think about your network in terms of the various places you meet and engage with others. Take a few minutes to answer the following questions:

- Who do I know from my current job or past positions?
- Who do I go to church/synagogue/temple with?
- Who lives in my neighborhood?
- Who do I know from alumni associations?
- Who were my childhood/college friends?
- What are my hobbies and who do I connect with?
- Who do I know from clubs or sports teams that I belong to?

- Who do I know from charities and non-profit organization affiliations?
- Who do I know who is part of my children's lives (such as, teachers or coaches or other parents)?
- Who do I know from any other aspects of my life?

Once you have completed this list, come back to it every few days for a couple of weeks. I guarantee you will add a few more names to your list each time. Then take a minute to open your checkbook or log-in to your online banking and follow where your money goes. Did you add your dentist, accountant, or hair dresser to your list? Any small business that you are already giving money to is automatically a powerful network. After all, you're already motivating these people by being a client.

Finally, look for holes or empty spaces in your network. Are you actively connected to people that share similar interests and goals? Do you know advisory support professionals such as attorneys, doctors, accountants, coaches and consultants? Do you know a great plumber or an honest and trustworthy realtor? All of these areas are important pieces of your network. Once you know who is already in your various networks you can gain a better picture of where you might want to branch out a bit and make some new connections.

Whether for filling holes in your network or for finding a steady vein of referral business to work, becoming an active part in a variety of different groups will help round out and anchor your network.

# Social Media Networking: 10 Tips for Financial Advisors

Are you new to social media? Not sure you're doing the right thing?

You already know it's about people. It's about connecting. It's about developing relationships.

Social media tools provide endless opportunities for individuals and businesses to network locally, nationally and internationally. Effective use of social media will help promote your services, locate business partners and service providers, and even get you hired. You can perform competitive analyses, monitor industry trends, establish yourself as an expert in your field, locate potential clients and customers, and recruit key hires.

The possibilities are endless, but how do you get started? Here are 10 tips financial advisors can use to start social media networking on the right track.

**1. Compliance matters.**
Before jumping into LinkedIn, Facebook, Twitter, Foursquare and so on… check with your compliance department first. Some broker dealers (BD) have accepted LinkedIn as the medium for social/business networking. Contact your BD. Don't ask, "Can I…?", but rather *"How* can I…?" If your firm doesn't have a written social networking usage document, get involved with creating

one. Volunteer as a test case. If approved, use LinkedIn to its fullest extent. We have capitalized on the opportunity and are now getting business inquiries and connecting with old and new customers.

**2. Early adopters.**
Now that compliance departments are beginning to allow social media participation, being an early user in your profession is a competitive advantage. Get started with your *Personal Profile* and include as much information as your BD allows. Start small; your page can evolve with time. Establishing a LinkedIn profile that includes your name and title is better than not having any profile at all!

**3. Your *Personal Profile*.**
A complete profile enables your audience to feel more comfortable about connecting. Don't be afraid to mention what you do in the community. Bring the human element into your profile. A few details about your volunteer work, personal life, and hobbies adds personality to your content and creates a whole picture of you as a person. Want to add more personality? Post a picture. When your audience knows your name and what you look like, they may feel more comfortable connecting with you. Strive for 100% completeness on your *Personal Profile* by adding your current position, at least two past positions, information about your education, a summary of your background/experiences, a profile photo, details about your specialties and at least three recommendations. Read the LinkedIn *Learning Center* (Home/More/Learning Center) or work through the instructions in the *Tools* at the bottom of the page and you'll learn that profiles completed 100% are weighted more heavily and rank higher in LinkedIn's internal search feature. Do you have a website? If so, be sure that your LinkedIn *Profile* mirrors your website profile.

**4. Your Company Profile.**
You can have only one personal LinkedIn *Profile* but, if your BD allows, you may also create a *Company Profile* which presents an opportunity to reveal the human

side of your company. Your *Company Profile* provides a peek at the individuals behind your brand, highlights how members use your products, and offers tools to bring your "brand" to life. When correctly used, this feature ties individual employees' profiles together and makes it easy for others to find and follow your company on LinkedIn. Your *Company Profile* should include a detailed company description, a list of specialties, links back to the company website, and profiles of current and former employees. You can showcase your business by adding descriptive product overviews with the *Services* tab. You will find instructions in *LinkedIn's Companies* section to add your *Company Profile* and information.

**5. Differentiate.**

The *Summary* section on your *Personal Profile* is an under-utilized area of many LinkedIn profiles. Use this section to describe your services, professional experience, goals and specialties. If you are an independent professional working for a company, this section should be used to provide visitors with what makes you stand out from the crowd. Scroll down a bit for the *Experience* section. This should resemble your resume and if you own your own firm or book of business, this area can help you further personalize and distinguish yourself. On your *Company Profile*, the *Overview* is your visitors' first chance to learn about your company and offers an opportunity to differentiate your business.

**6. Optimize Your Profile.**

Key words that will help you be "found" in a search are equally important on LinkedIn. Stay consistent with your messaging. Start your profile by creating a file of keywords approved by your BD. Create a list of your attributes and successes. Be sure to include your services or products and a list of their benefits. The keyword list should include business locations, demographics and personal interests. Obtain testimonial letters and recommendations (check with your compliance department if this is permissible and how to post as certain registrations have restrictions on the use of recommendations). Others will want to know what current and previous clients liked best about your services and why they would refer you to others. Including these keywords in the *Summary* and *Experience* sections of your profile increases the probability of being found by search engines. Did you know that the more you tweak your website and your LinkedIn profile, the chance that you will be recognized and found by search engines is improved? Finally, if you are an RIA or other independent, this keyword process can be used to assist in creating other marketing materials for your firm.

### 7. Are you a Resource?

With LinkedIn, you can provide your connections with the latest news and offerings from your company. Every time you post, your connections are alerted. Whether it is a new product or service offering, positive press, a recent award, LinkedIn helps you stay on the radar of a wide circle of friends, colleagues and acquaintances. As a service to your LinkedIn connections, email them informative links. You can be a resource in helping your clients and customers gain more visibility. If your company has a blog, ask your BD for permission to use LinkedIn's *Blog* application and connect to it.

Helpful content attracts connections and helps to differentiate you and your company. One of the great tools on LinkedIn is the *Answers* tool. Anyone on LinkedIn has the ability to post a question, on any topic. As an expert in your field, you can demonstrate your experience by answering the appropriate questions. If allowed by your BD, recommendations are an important part of your LinkedIn profile. LinkedIn suggests that users with recommendations are three times as likely to get inquiries through LinkedIn searches. To initiate a recommendation request, go to the Profile tab and select Recommendations. There you will find a list of your jobs and education and you can choose what you want to be recommended for, decide whom you'll ask, create your customized message and send from within LinkedIn.

### 8. Social Networking.

This is called social networking for a reason…be social. Join groups, financial magazines, or financial associations in order to connect with current clients, referrals, and prospects that might find you during their Internet travels. You can grow your list of LinkedIn connections through webmail contacts (email contacts who are already on LinkedIn), colleagues and classmates, and through networking on LinkedIn groups. Your connections are what make LinkedIn work for you, so taking the time to expand your reach is time well spent. Company "follows" make it possible for you to keep your eye on key events happening at companies you're interested in. LinkedIn *Groups* are a great way to stay on top of topics of interest to you and to network with others in your field. To find groups, go to *LinkedIn Groups Directory*. Also, be sure to include your LinkedIn URL in your email signature, on your website, your Facebook profile, any blogs your write, and especially on your print marketing collateral and business card.

## 9. Delegate.

Do you still have doubts about whether LinkedIn is a good use of your time? When I first started my LinkedIn *Profile*, I wasn't sure either. I suggest you do as I have; hire someone who knows more than you do about social networking. Or, you might designate one of your employees to manage an account or hire a writing professional to create your profile. Preparing an internet strategy for a competitive advantage in this area of marketing your company, products and services will pay off in the long run.

## 10. Rules, *yes* Rules!

LinkedIn has defined rules as to how to input our data. Your BD has defined rules of engagement with your clients. Don't cut corners or ignore the rules. I found this out the hard way. After spending hours posting information on my profile, it turned out the content was not compliance approved. The adage *"ask for forgiveness before asking for permission"* does not apply here. Following the rules is important. Discussing your objectives with your agency supervisor officer or compliance officer may save you time and embarrassment.

As you become more experienced in using LinkedIn for your business, you are likely to find a dozen other ways you can use LinkedIn to enhance your brand, your prospects and your revenues. Stay true to your beliefs and follow the guideline set by FINRA and your BD's social networking policy. I am convinced that using LinkedIn will help grow your practice or business. There will be new social networking freedoms granted to financial professionals in the future. Create, mold and plan your social media presence today and stay one step ahead of your competition.

# LinkedIn Profile Setup

It's surprising to me that there are so many professionals with incomplete or no LinkedIn profile. Originally thought of as a tool for job seekers, LinkedIn has become a prominent and important resource for business growth. A complete profile enables people - potential clients and potential new business connections - to check you out. It is common to meet people and then "Google" (when did this become a verb?) them to learn more and become familiar with the business. LinkedIn provides business owners and professionals with an immeasurable opportunity to enhance their networking success. It is simple and it's free. Let me repeat…it is simple to navigate and it's FREE! We can no longer be passive about how our clients, customers and potential relationships are using LinkedIn. Further, being a LinkedIn member will provide you and your firm with Google recognition and ranking, a tool to enhance online search for potential new business.

Your professional profile should include your previous experiences but most importantly, it should reflect your current situation and employment status. Although LinkedIn allows you to post your educational and work background, resist the urge to make it look like your online resume. Instead, focus on your strengths and in areas where you can help clients and potential clients solve their problems. Why are you the best accountant qualified to help them? What is your specific area of expertise? Position yourself as an expert in your field and optimize your presence by including articles you have written, awards and

## LinkedIn Profile Setup

recognitions earned, special skills, and post status updates that relate to your area of expertise.

We are working with several firms and businesses who are using social media for a range of purposes including client communications, thought leadership, recruiting, creating alumni networks, public relations, brand development, business development and employee communications. Firms should encourage its partners, associates, managers and other key employees who may be responsible for developing new business to set up a complete and robust LinkedIn profile.

LinkedIn has been identified as a valuable way to connect with prospects, clients and previous employees. Google searches are not limited to individuals, and more and more people are using LinkedIn to research companies. For example, a Google search of Barney Rubble, CPA of the firm Flintstone & Associates, will most likely show the Flintstone & Associates website and Barney Rubble's LinkedIn profile as the top two results. While your firm's website may expertly market your services and include staff bios, Barney Rubble's LinkedIn profile should represent him as a member of the firm and specifically show what value he, as individual, brings to the firm.

Your firm's legal staff, compliance and marketing departments should carefully craft a guidelines document for all social media involvement (not limited to LinkedIn). Your firm must have control over how the firm is represented in individual profiles, and assurance that disclosure of proprietary and client information is avoided. Encourage the use of LinkedIn by providing training to help employees establish their profile and get started making connections. Care should be taken in creating a LinkedIn profile that is complete and professional and has the interests of the firm in mind. I have worked with hundreds of staff at dozens of accounting firms and found that not much attention is given (by individuals and firms) to setting up professional LinkedIn profiles. I have created a list of the Top Ten Pitfalls of LinkedIn Profiles:

1. **Blank profile.** I see this a lot. Someone sets up a LinkedIn profile, but never takes the time to complete it. These profiles do not represent the individual or the company and even diminishes credibility.

2. **No photo.** Your professional photo allows the people you've met and previously worked with to quickly identify you. The photo should be a clear and professional headshot with only you in the picture. Many people find it far easier to remember a face than a name.

3. **Bad photo.** A picture of you sitting on a rock in front of a waterfall may be beautiful but doesn't suit the purpose, nor does a family photo or a picture of you and your buddies at a Giants' game. Also avoid cartoon images of yourself or a generic picture icon.

4. **Lacks a clear professional summary.** Your LinkedIn *Summary* is the first section of your profile and should clearly, accurately and briefly tell about your strengths, areas of expertise and the problems you can help clients and potential clients solve. This is your chance to provide an engaging description that highlights who you are and what you do—think of it as your 30-second elevator pitch.

5. **Lacks detailed professional expertise or specialty.** The Specialties field of your *Summary* allows you to list your areas of expertise that will help other users find you when they are looking for a specific skill-set or knowledge-base. What do you do that sets you apart? What is your value to the firm? Be specific, but avoid disclosing client information.

6. **Out of date.** When your profile does not reflect your current situation, no one benefits. Your professional experience is sorted in chronological order. Your position descriptions should use clear, succinct phrases to briefly explain what the company does and your main responsibilities and accomplishments.

7. **No recommendations.** Meaningful recommendations from partners and colleagues who work closest with you help illustrate your achievements, project credibility, and show why people enjoy working with you.

8. **Does not list skills.** The *Skills & Expertise* section of your profile is where you list keywords, or tags. This is helpful so that when people do a topical search, your profile can more easily be found.

9. **Does not link to company website.** A professional profile should include a link to the company website. It may also include a link to other social media outlets used.

10. **Not building a valuable network.** The first step in building a LinkedIn network is to upload a list of contacts from your Gmail, Hotmail, etc. accounts and from your Outlook and other contact files. Be choosy in building a network of contacts who relate to your industry, are also interested in business development, and who might add value to you or your other contacts. Avoid connecting with just anyone for the sake of increasing your number of contacts.

"LinkedIn is a social networking website for people in professional occupations. Founded in December 2002 and launched on May 5, 2003, it is mainly used for professional networking. As of June 2012, LinkedIn reports more than 175 million registered users in more than 200 countries and territories," (Wikipedia). LinkedIn offers some great resources to help set up profiles and learn to use LinkedIn as an effective business tool. Some of those resources can be found here:

- Learning Center: http://learn.linkedin.com/
- User Guide: http://learn.linkedin.com/new-users/
- Free LinkedIn Webinars: http://learn.linkedin.com/training/
- Business Development User Guide: http://learn.linkedin.com/business-development/

Regardless of your firm's size or focus, LinkedIn has emerged as a credible way to communicate brand and messaging. So don't hesitate to engage the use of LinkedIn for your accounting firm. Create a profile and build your connections!

# Marketing Strategies That Work

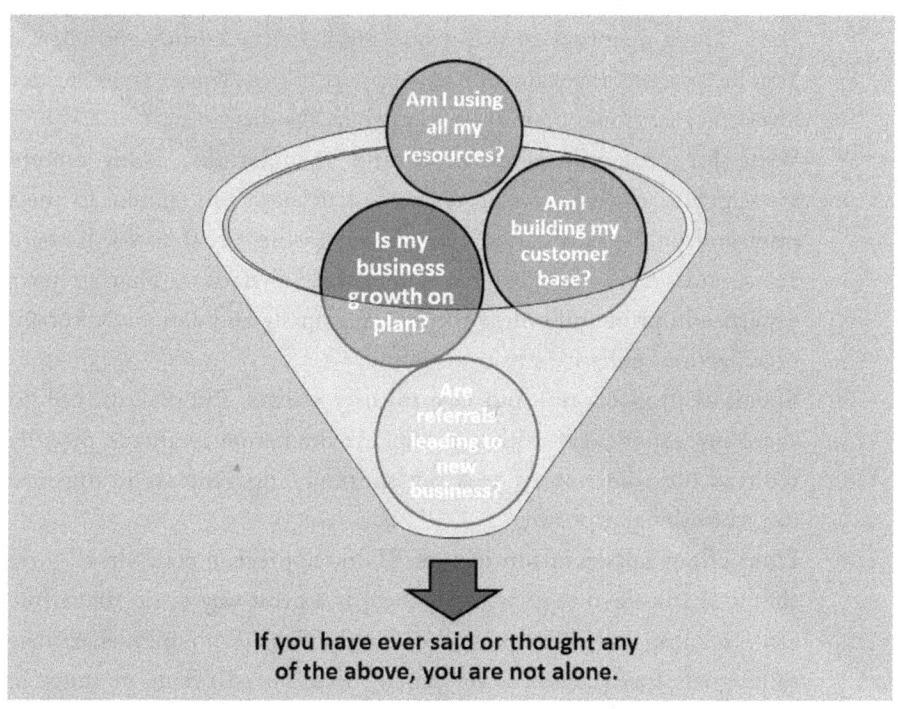

If you have ever said or thought any of the above, you are not alone.

We all find ourselves at a level of status quo from time to time. Plodding along. Not trying anything new. Stale. Over the years I have tried many different techniques and strategies to grow my business. They don't all work at the same time, and the fit has to be just right for where your business is today and where you want to take it next. Following are marketing strategies that have been successful for me. Keep this arsenal available to you for years to come.

**Proven marketing strategies that work:**

- **Establish a client-builder cluster group that meets each month.** Exchange information, introductions and endorsements with others interested in business development. I am currently involved in a group that has a mission to be a board of advisors. We gather monthly, all from different industries, to share our experiences and points of view. It is a small group of ten members, six of whom have been together for many years. Three members of this group are my close friends and clients. Together we are advocates for new opportunities. Would you consider investing four hours per month in a group like this?
- **Write for professional journals and associations.** Many editors are happy to receive your professional articles to add content to their print and online publications. Reach out to them first to see if there are submission guidelines that should be adhered to. Sharing your expertise in print and online through regionally and nationally known organizations enhance s your visibility.
- **Speak at professional and community events.** I never say "no" to share my experiences with a group. An invitation is always proudly received but sometimes I seek out speaking engagements to improve my professional exposure.
- **Host client appreciation events.** If you appreciate your clients, you should thank them regularly. An event is a great way to do that while also bringing together like-minded individuals who may share the same goals for business development. I've hosted events in suites at professional sporting events as well as an after work wine and cheese party at a local restaurant.
- **Sponsor a community event.** Sponsorship is a great way to get your name or your firm's name out there. Sponsor a 10K run or golf

tournament by providing giveaways, a monetary contribution, or signage.
- **Become credentialed.** Credentials always build credibility. If time and budget permit, try to obtain the next license or credential that is most pertinent in your field. Then make the announcement to prospects and clients.
- **Collect and share testimonials.** Whether they are offered to you or you specifically request a testimonial they can be used in many ways. Share testimonials in newsletters, on your website, in marketing materials, etc. Also, don't forget to thank the testimonial writer.
- **Be a connector.** If you can't solve a problem, refer your new contacts to people in your network who can. The benefit of this approach is twofold. First, you'll be seen as a problem solver, and second, those people who benefit from your referrals are more likely to provide you with referrals in return.
- **Volunteer.** The simple act of giving first is the single most important mindset transformation that you will need to build your business and follow your passion through relationship development. I do not share this advice so that you can put your financial contributions or the time commitment or even the achievement on display. Instead, I want you to see what the crucial element here really is: that giving of yourself, means a willingness to share your passion and your own unique gifts.
- **Plan to meet three new people each week in networking situations.** Set yourself this networking goal. Then go out there and connect with people at work, your children's sporting events, weddings, reunions, etc. You never know where a conversation may take you.
- **Identify and meet with a "mentor".** Mentoring happens when we ask for help from someone who has more experience with a particular body of knowledge than we do. Maybe you are unsure how to apply the information you are collecting. You may choose to seek out resources that can help you. Remember, one day you will be the expert and someone may ask for your help.

- **Send newsletters to prospects and clients.** There are online tools to help you collect contact information and create attractive and effective email newsletters. Check out Constant Contact or Mail Chimp.
- **Conduct informative seminars.** Conduct informational, technical, or instructional programs where you share the information your firm offers. This is a great way for prospects to "sample" your service and for clients to learn more. If you can offer continuing education credits, your attendees may be even more motivated to attend.
- **Take prospects to breakfast or lunch.** Breakfast and lunch are perfect for networking. If time is at a premium (and for most of us, it is), be sure to schedule in the morning for breakfast and at lunch. Not only will you find an extra hour or two in your day, but your connections may also appreciate the thought... and the extra time they will find in their day!
- **Send handwritten thank-you notes.** Once I realized its power in terms of relationship building, I became committed to this form of communication. I've made a habit of sending handwritten thank you notes and believe it is a vital strategy in both my business and personal lives.
- **Always carry business cards.** This may sound obvious, but I can't tell you how many networking events I attend where someone I've just met forgot to bring their cards. Hand them out freely everywhere you go.
- **Get to know assistants and receptionists.** Be professional, courteous and friendly. They are the gatekeepers to the decision makers.

# Conclusion

Let's face it, we are all networkers. We are born into a network: our family. We are graduates from high school and many of us go on to higher education, developing even more lifelong friendships from each of these areas: our personal network. I call on my network often (you do too) when I am looking for a good restaurant, doctor, plumber, travel destination, introductions for my children and a referral to a potential business relationship. I am also involved in my community, religious groups and neighborhood activities. If you do the same, good for you, keep it going and increase these activities. If you do not actively engage in this manner with you family, friends, community…start doing so now, it's never too late to help other people and create bonds.

## Conclusion

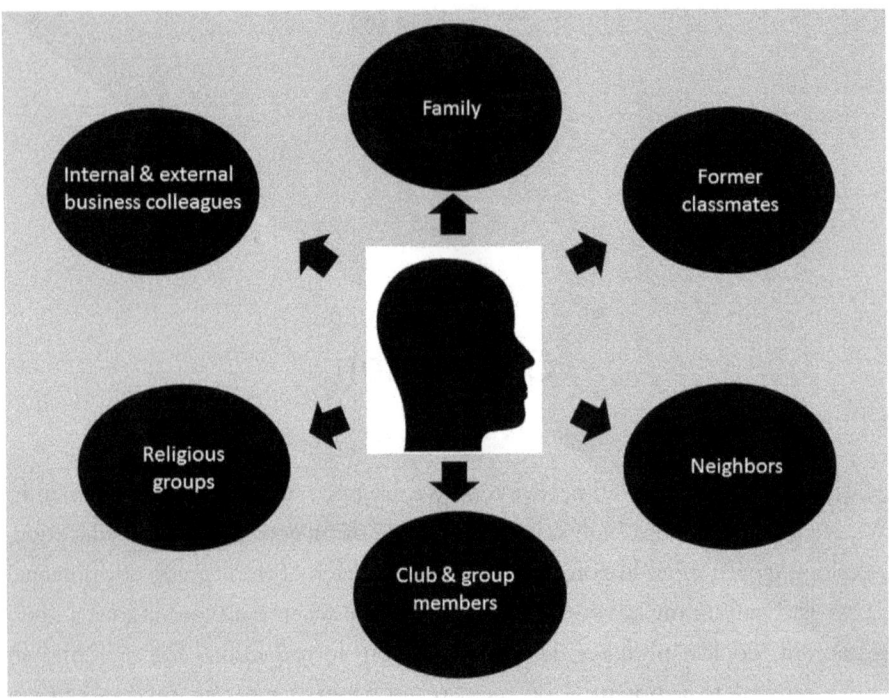

Realizing the potential for life changing results due to our activities around networking is the difference between successful relationship development and untapped, unrealized opportunities. Human beings are gregarious by nature; we need each other to grow, laugh, cry and prosper. It's the "human element" that creates these interactions.

This compilation of stories and articles is designed to help you realize your potential and recognize the opportunities to develop and nurture relationships that are present in your everyday life.

See yourself as a farmer who regularly plants seeds and enjoys the rewards of a thriving crop. Over the course of your lifetime, you are developing your network. Like the farmer's plants, your connections take shape to bear the nourishment needed for enduring, lifelong relationships. Continue to cultivate these relationships with a non-judgmental attitude, prune them and nurture them, and they will sustain you for the rest of your life.

Throughout my life, I can emphatically say that focusing on relationship development has rewarded me, my family, my co-workers and my employees. Each day I spend a little time thinking about how I can create a bond between myself and others or how I can create a bond between people that I care about and who I believe can help each other. Building bonds has rewarded me tenfold compared to the effort.

From this point forward, see yourself as a connector. See the relationships you spent a lifetime building as your "network" and a working template for growth, sharing and emotional intelligence.

Learn more about

**Creative Thinking**

by Andrew Bluestone:

HarnessingThePowerofRelationships.com

# Buy this book for your partners, salespeople or associates to give them:

- Real life examples that highlight the important aspects of their networks,
- "How-to" activities to overcome networking challenges,
- Strategies and tips to uncover opportunities and realize their potential,
- Steps to take that will develop new skills that become habits that translate into deeper, more significant relationships.

**Corporate volume discounts are available through HarnessingthePowerofRelationships.com**

www.ingramcontent.com/pod-product-compliance
Lightning Source LLC
Chambersburg PA
CBHW060157050426
42446CB00013B/2876